STOP NOTLEY

The Case for Throwing Out the NDP

SHEILA GUNN REID

About the Rebel

The Rebel.Media is a leading independent source of news opinion and activism. Launched by Ezra Levant and a group of dedicated Rebels after the Sun News Network shut down, The Rebel is essential for anyone looking for the other side of the story in conservative news, in Canada and across the world.

For more information about the Rebel, or more copies of this book, please go to www.TheRebel.Media.

TABLE OF CONTENTS

ACKNOWLEDGMENTS

Thank you to the Rebel staff for getting this book to print so quickly, to Ben Stanley for his editorial assistance and to all of our loyal Rebel supporters.

CHAPTER 1

THE DESTROYERS

Not long after Albertans woke up one terrible morning to realize they had lost control on election night and made their biggest mistake ever by marrying themselves to an NDP government, I wrote a book about the new team in charge. I called it *The Destroyers* because in that book I described in detail the anti-oil, anti-capitalist radical extremism of Premier Rachel Notley and the NDP. It was a book that made Rachel Notley furious: She would spend the next four years attacking me and The Rebel Media, where I work. I'll get into all that a bit later. The reason it made her so livid was pretty clear: I told Albertans the truth about her and her NDP government. And how they were out to destroy the proud, economically strong and free Alberta that generations had worked so hard to build.

Some people said they thought the title was an exaggeration. "Destroyers"? Really? Come off it, they said. Those NDPers are proud Albertans just like the rest of us. They want a strong economy. They want jobs for Alberta's workers. Maybe they're a bit further to the left on a few things, but how bad could they be?

As it turns out: They're worse than anyone imagined.

Even me.

After she was elected, Notley tried soothing the business community. Sure, she was a lefty and a paid-up member of the climate cult, she said. But things would be mostly business as usual, she said. "What I said very clearly during the campaign is that while we may believe there is some new consideration that needs to occur, that it will be done collaboratively and in partnership with our key job creators in this province," Notley said the day after her party's shock election victory. But she expected "they will come to realize things are going to be just A-OK over here in Alberta."

David Mowat, then the CEO of Crown-owned ATB Financial, predicted to the *Edmonton Journal* that he was guessing about the NDP that "they'll be surprisingly business friendly. I think their goal is to create stability in the province, and that's what the business community wants."

But things were not going to be A-OK. Not for businesses. Not for the oil patch. Not for investors. Not for workers. Not for taxpayers. The NDP did not turn out to be "business friendly" in the least. They instead handed unprecedented powers to unions, attacked family farms, ratcheted up minimum wages to record highs, cranked up taxes and even nationalized assets that previous governments had left to the private sector. The NDP did not "create stability in the province." On the contrary, Notley has overseen a period of turmoil worse than anything Alberta has seen since the bad old days of the National Energy Program: massive layoffs, dried up foreign investment, and businesses, workers and families fleeing the province.

No, things ended up being very far from "A-OK."

Just weeks after making that glib remark, in fact, Notley began turning the screws on the people of this great province and she hasn't let up since. She appointed Dave Mowat — Mr. "surprisingly business friendly" — to oversee a review of Alberta's oil and gas royalty system, creating immediate uncertainty for the industry and virtually paralyzing investment right off the bat, and it hasn't recovered since. Then she raised business taxes. And personal taxes. And announced —

surprise! — a carbon tax, which she never once mentioned during her election campaign. And she was just getting warmed up. Over the past four years under Rachel Notley, Alberta went from being one of the most stable, investment-friendly jurisdictions in the world, to being the most toxic province in the country for investors and businesses.

One regret that I had about my first book, and I wrote about it at the time, was that it came too late. The NDP had already been elected. We were stuck. The media, the other parties, and yes, the voters — we all should have done a far better job scrutinizing Notley's team of radicals long before we let them anywhere near the corridors of power. Now that her term is ending, and there's an election coming (and not a moment too soon) we can finally stop them. We can't screw this up again. We just can't. Albertans are barely hanging on as it is. Another four years under Notley's anti-oil, anti-business socialists, and this province may never recover. I truly believe that — and I bet you do, too.

But, for those who are still in denial, who still believe this is a normal government, and that Notley was just dealt a bad hand, this book is guaranteed to set them straight. The NDP government hasn't done the best that it could in the face of low oil prices and hostile governments in other provinces and in Ottawa; It's made everything far, far worse. Rachel Notley has had some turns of bad luck, sure, but that's not her biggest problem. Her biggest problem is that her NDP party aren't actually proud Albertans just like the rest of us. So, before we begin our march through the smoking ruin and destruction that the NDP inflicted on Alberta over the last four years, I'm going to recap some of what I covered in *The Destroyers* as a reminder of who these people really are.

So if you've already read *The Destroyers* (and you could well be — it was No. 1 on Amazon.ca and is likely the bestselling Alberta political book of all time) the rest of this chapter might seem familiar to you. So feel free to jump ahead, if you prefer. But if you haven't heard yet or you need a refresher about the people inside Rachel Notley's inner circle, and just how radically anti-business, anti-oil and anti-Albertan they were from the very start, then you'll want to read on.

Is Rachel Notley anything like the Albertans you know? For years Notley has been walking into Alberta's legislature — the seat of the province's democracy — wearing a wristwatch with the face of Che Guevera, the Marxist who helped lead the Cuban communist revolution and served as a minister under Fidel Castro. Like communists everywhere, he was also a brutal murderer of anyone who he thought was an enemy of the cause. Thomas Lukaszuk, a former MLA whose family defected from Communist Poland, once told Notley how "hurtful it is" for her to glorify one of the darlings of a system that brutally oppressed and murdered so many millions of people. She didn't seem to care.

Notley isn't a moderate. She's not a liberal. She's not a left-wing Albertan. She's an old-school international socialist. She's a crusader from the international labour movement. Her husband, Lou Arab, is even the communications officer for the Canadian Union of Public Employees, the same union that has campaigned against Canada's fight against the Islamic State; that accuses Israel of "unjust and disproportionate violence" in its defence against rocket attacks from Gaza; and most recently has supported Venezuela's socialist tyrant Nicolas Maduro, despite the Canadian government refusing to recognize his rigged election and his corrupt rule.

Say this about the socialists in Venezuela: At least they like their country's oil industry (too much, in fact: after former president Hugo Chavez forced out private foreign investors and seized oil assets, he ended up running his country's oil industry into the ground; Notley's husband sure has a type!)

Notley has run Alberta's oil into the ground because she never liked it; she's never supported it. Before she was elected, Notley warned that "unfettered development" of the oilsands is bad for the province. "Slow down the expansion," she said, until oilsands companies clean up their environmental act. She calls their tailings ponds "toxic tailings lakes," even though the same kind of tailings ponds are used by other resource industries, like mining, as are used by the oilsands. Oh, did I say "oilsands"? That's not the term she used. Before she was premier, Notley preferred to call them "tar sands," to make them sound that much dirtier.

For her whole career before she was premier, Notley was the voice in the legislature for the anti-oil activists. Not long before the NDP's election, Notley actually attended a rally where protestors carried signs reading "no tar sands, no tankers, no pipelines." When she was in opposition, one of her staffers was a Greenpeace activist who stormed into a dinner held for the then-premier, to protest against government support for the oil industry. She opposed Keystone XL and Northern Gateway pipelines even after they were approved by the National Energy Board. She was more hardcore anti-pipeline than even Prime Minister Justin Trudeau. And she said she wants to put the brakes on hydraulic fracturing of shale, or fracking — which we've been doing in Alberta for decades.

So it's no wonder that one of Notley's most important advisers was Brian Topp, who she made her chief of staff shortly after her election. Topp is unabashedly anti-pipeline. He's unashamedly anti-oilsands. He's vehemently anti-coal. He's proudly anti- every fossil fuel that comes out of Alberta's sediment. He's said Canada "should produce a great deal less hydrocarbon energy." Of course, why should he care if that also means "a great deal less" jobs in the hydrocarbon industry? Topp doesn't come from Alberta. He didn't even live here, until Notley took power and paid him $200,000 a year to be her top operative. Topp's a union leader from Toronto. He's even represented the NDP at Socialist International meetings in Europe. He even threw his support behind the anti-capitalist Occupy movement. In Notley's mind, that apparently qualifies him to run the Alberta government.

So the premier's top hire ended up being a guy who complained that the pro-energy policies of the Alberta and federal governments are "blighting the rest of our economy." Before he moved to Alberta, he was trying to help get B.C.'s provincial NDP elected on an anti-pipeline platform, as their campaign manager (in 2017, the B.C. NDP were able to narrowly secure power, and they've been blocking Alberta's pipeline efforts ever since).

Topp has argued for a "legally binding ban on oil tankers" off the northwest coast of B.C. — which the federal Liberal government ended up acting on, thus blocking any possible pipeline to tidewater that might run up there. In 2011, Topp told the Vancouver-area *Georgia*

Straight newspaper that he was dead-set against the proposed Keystone XL pipeline, too. Economic "madness" is what he called it. "Let's be clear, I think it should be stopped," he said of the Keystone XL pipeline. "It is a fundamentally wrong economic choice and a wrong environmental choice with enormous consequences ... all across the country." As it turns out, the biggest consequences to Alberta and the country has been a lack of pipelines to export our oil, forcing its price down to abysmal lows, thanks to the ongoing anti-pipeline work of Notley, Topp and their friends.

Topp once ran for the leadership of the federal NDP, but he was considered too radical. During one leadership debate, he actually said he wanted to force "fossil-fuelled cars out of our cities." In his platform for the leadership, he vowed to "Develop a national energy strategy to transition Canada to a low-carbon economy and limit the impacts of oil sands development during the transition." He's compared Canada's oil industry to the arms industry. Ethical oil? He scoffs at it. "Let's get into ethical landmines," he's quipped — to him, they're equally unethical.

Topp is also a fan of policies like "what they're doing in Europe," he says, which he says includes: "a hard cap on emissions, to price carbon, a home and industrial retrofit program, getting out of coal, getting an urban mass-transit program, and getting fossil-fuelled cars out of our cities." That, he said, has "got to be at the heart" of government policy here. In 2016, Topp left Notley's office and headed back to Toronto, but he left behind his plan for emission caps, carbon prices and coal shutdowns that had indeed become the heart of the NDP's government policy.

And they've been ripping at the heart of Alberta ever since.

This is how the Notley NDP earned being called "destroyers." They took a situation where Alberta already faced challenges, because of falling oil prices, and took away everything that should have helped the province weather the tougher times. Were any investors looking to capitalize on low oil prices by buying undervalued companies, or starting up new ones more cheaply, or investing in discounted assets, the NDP scared them off with a whole suite of anti-oil, anti-business measures like the carbon tax, emission caps, unnecessary royalty reviews, more regulation and higher taxes on businesses and workers. They turned Alberta from a magnet for international capital into a province that repels investment. And it's not by accident: It's what their hard-left, carbon-hating leaders, including Notley and Topp, had promised to do all along, if only more people had paid attention.

I mean, one of their top cabinet ministers, Shannon Phillips, even helped write a book on how to fight capitalism. She's now environment minister and she's fighting capitalism every day now by making investors and businesses her government's target for attack. "A democratic society doesn't just condone political action," Phillips and her co-worker, the environmental extremist Mike Hudema wrote in the introduction to their 2004 book *An Action a Day Keeps Global Capitalism Away.* "It demands it."

They celebrated any action it might take to stop capitalists, including a "blockade" on a road, much like the ones pipeline opponents have been using to stop Alberta from exporting its oil. Or, they added, "Greenpeace militants climbing to the top of a building to drop a banner" — like the Greenpeace militants that have sabotaged oil projects in Alberta. Mike Hudema is actually a Greenpeace activist himself. He's literally broken into worksites to "occupy" them as a way to protest Alberta's oil sector. He hung from a bridge to try stopping the Trans Mountain pipeline expansion project. This is the guy who's good friends with Alberta's environment minister; who wrote book with her celebrating the destructive things Hudema has been doing to hurt Alberta's working families.

Phillips put plenty of hard work herself into "political action" to hurt Alberta's economy and industry before the NDP was elected, and she traded guerrilla action against Alberta's industry for government action. She personally succeeded in a campaign to stop a natural gas production project in Lethbridge. She argued back in 2012 against the rapid expansion of the valuable oilsands resource, "The benefits of slowing development far outweigh the risks," she wrote. In 2008, she travelled to Fort McMurray with Al Jazeera, the terror-promoting Qatari state broadcaster, to film an unflattering documentary on the oilsands. At a conference in 2013, she sat on a panel at a media conference that argued that the oilsands are "the source of the country's fastest-growing carbon emissions, and are having a significant impact on provincial and federal democracy, human and treaty rights, and the social fabric." She sat on another panel that year in Ottawa to argue that the oilsands "hurts women." Phillips was a big backer of the Kyoto Accord. She complained about Alberta's "rapidly antiquating approach to the environment and climate change" and called Alberta "a province that pays the bills by pumping CO2 into the atmosphere." And before getting elected here, she helped work to try getting her anti-pipeline allies in the B.C. NDP elected next door.

And those are just the biggest names in the NDP government's anti-capitalist caucus. I haven't even gotten into Rod Loyola, unofficial president of the NDP's Hugo Chavez fan club. "Long live Hugo Chavez. Long live the values that he stood for," Loyola declared in a video on his YouTube channel (he's since tried to block it). When Chavez died in 2013, Loyola organized a vigil for him, calling it "an opportunity to express solidarity with the Venezuelan people and support for the Bolivarian Revolution" and to "share with the media and local community the hard work, dedication and achievements of President Hugo Chávez and his government." Loyola has characterized Alberta's oil and gas industry as colonial oppressors, telling Edmonton's *VUE Weekly* magazine in 2014 that First Nations need to "defend themselves from these (capitalist) economic systems and the oppression that those economic systems have created," Loyola said.

When Hugo Chavez died in 2013, Loyola wrote on his Facebook page that Canada could learn a lot from his authoritarian communist leadership, "especially regarding democracy and social and economic justice." You know, the justice in Venezuela where political opponents of the regime that Loyola so admires are being locked up or killed. The place that used to be the richest in South America but now people can't get food or medicine because the maniacal Marxist ideology of Chavez and his successors have destroyed the economy. Alberta could learn a lot from that?

Or there's Graham Mitchell, who was parachuted in by Brian Topp from his far-left drum-circle network in Toronto to be chief of staff in the Alberta energy ministry. Mitchell used to run a hard-core left-wing anti-resource group called LeadNow, which, under Mitchell, ran television ads denouncing the Conservative government's support for the oil industry. ("The Harper government has stripped out our environmental protections ... and damaged our international reputation. They've taken our country backwards," the narrator of the ad says, as the video shows crude black oil being spilled over forests and rivers, with the words "TAR SANDS," "PIPELINES" and "SUBSIDIES TO OIL AND GAS" flashed on the screen in dark tones.) He was also a director at the federal NDP think tank, the Broadbent Institute, where he actually trained other lefty activists to campaign against Alberta's oil and gas. And just days before he took the job at Alberta's energy ministry, Mitchell was still a registered lobbyist pushing Ottawa for tighter restrictions on Alberta's oil industry.

Or there's Colin Piquette, who has written and acted out political performance theatre that attacks Canada's resource industries — in his retelling, we were "The Republic of Greedolia," and Piquette appeared alongside a defaced Canadian flag: Turned upside-down, it had the words "No Justice on Stolen Land" scrawled on it. He said he can't be proud of Alberta. "How can you?" he asked at a protest rally backing First Nations against government and industry, where people carried signs that read "Genocide in Our Backyards" and "No Blood for Oil" and another inverted, defaced Maple Leaf flag that read "Canada: Stop Denying Your Holocaust."

Or there's Dave Mowat, the guy the NDP hired to run their royalty review. Remember, he was the one who said we could expect the NDP to be "surprisingly business friendly" because "their goal is to create stability in the province." Mowat actually trained as a disciple of Al Gore, to become an "environmental warrior" — an official Al Gore representative in the global campaign to spread the anti-oil message of Gore's propaganda film, An Inconvenient Truth. And he was an enthusiastic backer of the Tides Foundation, the billionaire-funded organization that has devoted itself to shutting down Alberta's oil industry, with campaigns like the "Week to End Enbridge" and the anti-export "Tanker Free Coast campaign."

And that's still just to name a few of the most reckless, radical socialists that have been running roughshod for the past four years over Alberta's once-vibrant economic powerhouse. Albertans literally elected a hostile power to run the province, an enemy of our industry, of our workers, of investors and of the Alberta we and our families have built and love. The union organizers and community campaigners that make up this NDP government have never built anything in their lives. They wouldn't know how to. As we've all seen to our horror over the last four years, all these NDPers know how to do is … destroy.

CHAPTER 2

"NO LONG TERM FUTURE IN THE TAR SANDS"

Albertans know that one of the biggest problems strangling the province's economy is the lack of pipelines to export our oil. That's what led to producers sitting on such a glut of oil that simply couldn't find its way out of the province that by late 2018, the discount on Alberta oil over comparable U.S. oil had grown to as much as US$52 a barrel. Producers were losing a fortune, up to $100 million a day. The rest of us were losing, too: Hundreds of millions of dollars in royalties and taxes because of a lack of pipelines are lost forever and have to be made up at some point by other taxes — our taxes. Notley ended up ordering producers to "curtail" their production starting January 1, 2019. That means she ordered them to actually slow down their production just to add to the glut and keep prices from falling further, which would inevitably cost jobs. She announced that the province would be buying railcars — more taxpayer cash required for that, too. What Notley didn't mention that she was a big reason why this economic disaster happened in the first place.

You see, Rachel Notley was anti-pipeline before it was cool. Long before John Horgan was elected the NDP premier of British Columbia,

Notley was already showing him how to oppose pipelines through B.C. Before Justin Trudeau decided that we shouldn't have Energy East and buried the proposal under endless new regulatory burdens and changes, Rachel Notley was already against the idea.

Remember when Justin Trudeau announced that he would ban all oil tankers from carrying Alberta crude to the coast of Northern B.C. and that he was outlawing the previously approved Northern Gateway pipeline proposal because, he said, a pretty B.C. rainforest "is no place for a pipeline"? Notley was way ahead of him on both fronts.

In April 2015, less than a month before she would take power, Notley spelled out why she was against Northern Gateway. She said the proposed pipeline was "not the right decision." She even promised to "rescind" the Alberta government's official support from it if she were elected. "There's too much environmental sensitivity there and there's genuine concern by the Indigenous communities," she said. Why, that's exactly the language opponents have used against every Alberta pipeline proposal. When did it become the Alberta premier's job to decide on the "environmental sensitivity" in another province? (Maybe it's connected to the fact that Notley's environment minister, Shannon Phillips, before she was elected actually attended National Energy Board hearings to argue against Northern Gateway's approval.)

And when did it also become the Alberta premier's job to worry about Indigenous communities who are not only in another province, but whose concerns are constitutionally an issue that the federal government is responsible for, not the provinces? As it happens most of the "Indigenous communities" affected by the Northern Gateway plan actually supported the plan. And the National Energy Board had already ruled that the environmental impact was acceptable. So what on earth was Notley talking about? Why was someone looking to govern a province that relies on pipelines scrounging for lame excuses to "rescind" the Alberta government's support for such a crucial one?

Probably because she wanted to give cover to the federal Trudeau Liberals for pulling the plug on Northern Gateway — which they did, one year later, citing the same weak reasoning that Notley used. Only now, Indigenous groups are actually mad because they wanted those tankers and pipeline. They're even trying to sue Ottawa over the decision, which cost them jobs, equity and economic opportunities — think about that: Aboriginals going to court to demand a pipeline, rather than stopping one. And Notley's government even managed to blow that pipeline. Maybe the Indigenous groups should have their lawyers come after Notley for giving Trudeau the idea to kill Northern Gateway in the first place.

She even admitted that she helped nudge Trudeau toward narrowing the list of proposed pipelines to just the Trans Mountain expansion. Trans Mountain happened to be the one pipeline that happens to run right through the suburbs of green-obsessed Vancouver, and was always therefore bound to be a magnet for the most vicious protests and blockades. But that's the one Notley told Trudeau to chase. Right after he was elected, a few months after she became Alberta premier, Notley explained: "We said that we needed one of those pipelines to go west and that we would work with them to get one of those pipelines to go west. We are now working with them to get one of those pipelines to go west." Like Trudeau, she wasn't interested in increasing the maximum number of pipelines, running west, south, east, north, up, down — whatever it takes to get the maximum amount of Alberta oil out of the province at the best price. She was interested in winnowing down the options to the fewest possible.

And once the federal government finally decided to let Alberta have maybe just that one pipeline — if we're lucky, that is — Notley was advising the federal Liberals to take a hands-off approach to getting it approved and built. Back in 2017, when governments in B.C. were making mischief for the Trans Mountain plan, back when it was still owned by Kinder Morgan, Notley was initially saying she didn't want Ottawa to get involved. "We know the federal government has made the decision that the project is to go ahead. That's what we needed to have happen," she said, after the city of Burnaby started refusing to issue building permits to Trans Mountain as a way of stymying the project. But that was all Ottawa needed to do, she said. "You have to respect the role of the NEB to a certain degree, so if you push too hard and you undermine the process such that it then becomes subject to challenge, that's not helpful either." Eventually the risks of so much mischief led to Kinder Morgan walking away from Trans Mountain, and the federal government having to buy the whole thing. Has anyone ever been more wrong about one thing than Notley has been about Alberta's pipeline needs?

Even where she couldn't find fake excuses about environmental sensitivity and Indigenous concerns, Notley was still willing to fight pipelines with anything she could come up with. The Keystone XL pipeline that Alberta's oil producers have been desperately trying to get to increase export capacity to the U.S. wasn't going through any B.C. rainforests. There were no B.C. First Nations to worry about. The only thing stopping it had been former president Barack Obama's pandering to U.S. environmentalists, without caring about the impact on Albertans or Canadians, who don't get to vote for the president anyway.

Well, Obama and Rachel Notley. Because, like the former U.S. president, the premier was always making the case against Keystone XL, too. "We're against it," she had said, over and over again. Rob Merrifield, Alberta's former envoy in Washington, D.C. said "the Premier's first directive" while he was in that post, after she was elected, was to "stop all KXL lobby(ing)." Publicly, Notley said it was because she didn't want Alberta shipping "unprocessed bitumen" to the U.S.: "if we ship unprocessed bitumen to Texas, according to this government and to the American government, we will give tens of thousands of Alberta jobs to Texas — not to Albertans — and that's not what Albertans want to see," Notley said.

Of course, shipping unprocessed bitumen to the U.S. is exactly what Albertans have been desperate to see. It's the very thing Notley would end up buying millions of dollars' worth of rail cars in 2018 to help make happen. And curtailing production just to free up the limited pipeline space available, thanks to opposition to Keystone XL and Northern Gateway by Notley and her peers. Save the talk about "processing" bitumen until the day an investor actually sees a better economic opportunity in building an upgrader in Alberta than building pipelines out of Alberta. But this province built its economy and its prosperity on producing oil and gas, not processing them. Blocking a pipeline in the name of diversifying the economy is just another of Notley's excuses for blocking pipelines.

Because regardless of what Notley says about supporting pipelines now, the reason Alberta's in this position is in large part because she helped give cover to the anti-pipeline forces working to landlock Alberta by being the first premier ever elected who actually opposed more export capacity for Alberta oil. And Notley's long been against more pipeline capacity for Alberta's oil because she's really against Alberta continuing to produce oil. Even after she was elected premier, she was still telling the world that Alberta would be getting out of the oil business. In a September 2015 article with the helpful headline "No long-term future in tar sands, says Alberta's premier" in the U.K.'s left-wing *The Guardian* newspaper, Notley made it clear she thought the oilsands needed to go. "Notley also forecast an eventual future beyond fossil fuels," the reporter explained, quoting the premier: "I don't think we are defined by energy. Certainly in the short to medium term that is an asset that we have, so we have to look at how we develop it carefully and responsibly because of the obligation we have to the people employed in the industry," she told *The Guardian*. "Do I see that as our reason for being 100 years from now? Well, I hope we will have learned a lesson of diversification by then." In other words, if it weren't for the mass unemployment it would cause, she would shut down the oil industry today. Never mind the economic benefits. Never mind that oil is a product the world needs more of every day and no one produces it more ethically than Albertans do. Let the world buy its oil from Saudi Arabia and Venezuela, as far as she's concerned. Alberta needs to learn a lesson by getting out of a highly profitable business where we have a natural advantage, and diversifying instead into ... more government jobs, I guess?

Notley drove away tens of billions of dollars in oil and gas investment from Alberta. But as the 2019 election approached, she was desperate for proof that she hadn't turned Alberta into a business wasteland. She needed to show that someone — anyone — thought that the Alberta oil patch was still a good bet under Notley.

So in January, Rachel Notley announced that she was giving a $440-million loan guarantee to a Calgary-based company called Value

Creation that was supposed to be building a massive new oil sands upgrader near Edmonton. She made a big deal about it. She held a press conference where she was joined Dr. Columba Yeung, the president and majority owner of Value Creation.

Notley celebrated it as a way to add value, to diversify, to build up Alberta's upgrading capacity and create jobs.

Here's what she said in the press release: "Calgary-based Value Creation Inc. (VCI), and its wholly-owned subsidiary Value Chain Solutions Inc., is on track to invest $2 billion in an upgrading facility in the Alberta Industrial Heartland, just east of Edmonton, which will create more than 2,000 construction jobs and another 200 full-time positions once the facility is up and running."

It sounded great. Except the whole thing was a lie.

Notley made the announcement at a press conference. Reporters dutifully gave her the positive media coverage she wanted. It looked like a great day for Notley — because it proved that she could get massive investments in the oil patch, and that construction is already underway on this amazing new upgrader.

But none of it was true.

After the announcement, I wanted to check it out. The project site for this supposed upgrader just happens to be down the road from where I live. So I went to see it. And guess what? There was no activity there at all. There was no construction already underway. There was no construction at all.

What I saw were a lot of vacant fields. It looked like there was some construction at some point a long time ago, maybe 10 years back, but then it was abandoned. It looked like no one has put a shovel in the ground in a decade.

The Rebel even phoned the industrial park where this abandoned property is located, and the managers didn't even know what we were talking about at first. They were so unfamiliar with it, they had to look it up. Eventually they confirmed that Value Creation did own the land, but that nothing had been done with the property in years.

But Rachel Notley specifically said that construction was "underway". Why would she lie?

And anyone could see something was fishy just by visiting the website of the company, vctek.com. Other than a copy of Rachel Notley's announcement, nothing had been updated on there for years. If you clicked on their news release page: Nothing. If you clicked on their "recent events" page: Nothing. When we clicked on their "careers" page to apply online for a job, it was actually broken. "Not Found," it said. We kept checking back for weeks after the announcement. It wasn't fixed.

So Rachel Notley says construction is underway and they're about to hire 2,000 people — but their website's job application is broken?

The Rebel called the company — which apparently all the reporters at the CBC and the rest of the mainstream media swallowing Notley's PR couldn't be bothered to do — and asked some basic questions about what's really going on.

The spokesperson there, Iva Georgieva, told us that Value Creation doesn't actually have any operations. "Right now, operations in Alberta? No," she said. She said they have "oilsands resources" — presumably meaning a lease on some oil land — and a "planned demonstration plant in High River." And she said "we have partially built our upgrader in (the) industrial heartland."

So no operations. A vacant lot sitting there useless, for 10 years. Where exactly is this company getting $2 billion to spend on this fabled upgrader that Notley was touting?

Georgieva couldn't say. But when The Rebel did some digging, we found out something interesting: a news story from exactly 10 years earlier that reported on an oilsands company called BA Energy filing for bankruptcy protection. The report said "The company and its parent company, Value Creation Inc. (VCI) is struggling to stay afloat after halting construction on a massive upgrader project. BA is suffering from a cash flow shortage and as such will be unable to repay a loan of approximately $50-million plus interest to VCI due Dec. 31, 2008, said BA chairman and CEO Columba Yeung in an affidavit filed Dec. 29 with the Alberta Court of Queen's Bench."

So they are a real company. But they became insolvent 10 years ago. The article confirms they halted construction. Ten years ago. Nothing's underway. Rachel Notley lied.

And look at the credit history of this company that Notley is about to give a $440 million loan guarantee — guaranteed with Alberta taxpayer money. Value Creation had to repay a $50 million loan back on December 31, 2008, but it ran to court two days before it was due and told a judge it couldn't pay.

Columba Yeung was the same guy standing next to Notley when she was beaming about putting taxpayer dollars at risk for this mysterious upgrader. But read his sworn affidavit from when he was trying to get out from repaying another loan just 10 years ago. Remember that VCI stands for "Value Creation Inc.," which is the parent company of BA Energy, and the company that Notley's getting into bed with:

"BA Energy is suffering from a cash flow shortage and as such will be unable to repay a loan (as defined below) of approximately $50 million plus interest to VCI due December 31, 2008. The failure to repay the loan may place VCI in default of its main credit facility thus permitting the credit facility lenders (as defined below) to accelerate repayment and immediately demand the full balance owing on the VCI PIK Loan, which will, as of January 9, 2009, amount of approximately US$507 million."

It goes on like that for a long time. Yeung was asking the court to protect his company from creditors who wanted to be repaid US$507 million.

Things were tough back then, with the 2008 financial crisis, and Yeung's partial bitumen upgrader idea wasn't selling. He told the judge his technology was really, really good, and when oil prices were better maybe someone would invest in them. As he wrote: "While the VCI Technology is not currently in use, there is substantial evidence to support my contention that it will revolutionize oil sands upgrading processes and become and economical technology even at today's pricing for crude." This is the technology that Notley was betting on.

But Yeung swore that affidavit back when the price of oil was $35 a barrel in December of 2008. But in 2009, the price of oil really came back. It actually doubled in price. And by mid-2011, the price of oil had tripled. It was more than $100 a barrel. Still, nobody was investing in Yeung's technology. Serious companies came to investigate it — but none of them thought it worked. One retired oilsands CEO from a multi-billion-dollar company told The Rebel that Yeung "spent the last 15 years trying to convince all serious refining players that his technology of partial upgrading is the answer to all problems. It would have been if it only worked. Total, Shell, BP etc. (They) all looked at his technology but none believe it will work. Suppose it is easier to convince the NDP."

So Yeung borrowed US$507 million and defaulted, and sought creditor protection (he told The Rebel he did his best to repay the banks and there's no reason to assume otherwise). His website appears to have been dormant, because nobody was backing his play. Until Rachel Notley came around, with a promise of $440 million — of your money and mine.

And when The Rebel contacted Yeung, he confirmed what we had suspected: They're not actually working anything. They don't in fact have construction underway. And he actually told us that his project is not at the stage where it would even make sense to raise money for it.

Well, that's confusing. Rachel Notley specifically said construction was already underway. There's no construction underway. Rachel Notley specifically said they were on track to raise $2 billion dollars. There's no money that's lined up. There's no upgrader.

Rachel Notley lied.

She destroyed the oil patch. And now she's having fake press conferences to pretend otherwise.

CHAPTER 3

"EMBARRASSING COUSINS"

Before Notley's NDP was elected in May 2015, few people noticed how long her party had been down on Alberta. They don't really like the province all that much. They're embarrassed to be Albertan. They actually came out and said so.

Brian Mason, formerly the NDP leader and now a cabinet minister, called the oilsands industry an "environmental embarrassment" (except he used the name "tar sands," the same one preferred by anti-Alberta propaganda groups as a way to make our oil sound extra dirty). Brian Topp, who would become Premier Notley's first chief of staff, said that the way Alberta manages its resources is "blighting the rest of (Canada's) economy." Then there was Shannon Phillips, who would become environment minister in Notley's government, who appeared at an Ottawa panel on gender to tell the country that Alberta's energy-based industry was hurting women, and how it was somehow also bad for the Central Canadian manufacturing economy. Oh, and don't forget Colin Piquette, one of Notley's MLAs, saying he couldn't bring himself to "be proud of where I'm from."

You would think that after campaigning for the privilege of leading this great province, and winning, they would at least be proud now.

After all, Albertans, for better or worse, were at least willing to trust the NDP to show us how they might improve things, by actually putting them into power. But prejudices run deep. And even once they took over government, the NDP just couldn't stop themselves from trashing our province and condescending to the very people they're supposed to be representing.

It didn't even take long after the election for that contempt to surface once again. In September 2015, just a few months after becoming premier, Notley sat down with *Global News* to be part of a puff-piece program billing her as a "Woman of Vision." It should have been an easy, three-minute, free advertisement for her and the NDP, a chance to say lots of great things about herself and the province she was fortunate enough to be leading. Instead, she couldn't help but trash talk Alberta in front of a national audience, saying that she foresaw a day, under her leadership, when Alberta could be "proud" instead of being "an embarrassing cousin that no one wants to talk about."

Of course, outside the NDP offices, Albertans are already pretty damn proud. And who does she really believe it is that thinks of Alberta as an "embarrassing cousin," anyway? No doubt that's the prevailing view among the café socialists on Vancouver Island, or on Queen Street West in Toronto. And I guess in Justin Trudeau's Liberal caucus, too. But are those the people we want to impress? Does Notley really think that view is widely shared among normal, hardworking people across Canada? Does she truly think that the average man or woman on the street in Halifax or Thunder Bay or Flin Flon or Saskatoon is "embarrassed" by Alberta? On the contrary, a lot of them have probably thought about moving to Alberta. Certainly a whole lot of them were moving here before Notley became premier: from 2011 to 2014, tens of thousands of people were flocking to the province. Some embarrassment.

Amazingly, even after she was widely assailed for slagging our province on a national stage like that, Notley didn't apologize. She didn't relent. She stood by it. She doubled down. Albertans needed to hear the hard truth about just how embarrassing they are, she suggested. "Rhetorical boosterism that suggests everything is just fine interferes with that well-informed, thoughtful conversation that Albertans need to have," she said.

That condescension for Alberta and the dismissal of any justifiable pride in this province would set the tone for Notley's next four years. Time and time again, the NDP would make it clear that they didn't much like Albertans and the choices that Albertans had made in building this province.

Like when Notley tries defending her carbon tax. Notley whacked Alberta families, businesses and even non-profits and schools with a painful extra tax right when the economy was at its weakest, but don't complain to her about it. It's your fault, she says. You see, Albertans have all been making the wrong choices about the way they use energy. And Notley will see to it that they see the error of their ways and correct themselves and follow her NDP right-think. "Once it (the carbon tax) comes into play, they'll see that it actually is a tremendous opportunity for them to make better choices," she said. Better choices — meaning the choices she wants you to make. And she means a tremendous opportunity in the way that losing your job gives you more free time to catch up on your reading. She just wants to tax us until we discover the opportunities to make the choices she thinks are better for us, the misguided, ungrateful people of Alberta.

And what are those "better choices," you might ask? Oh, just the tremendous opportunity to be cold, uncomfortable and inconvenienced. When a reporter in a 2016 press conference dared to ask Notley about the extra burden a carbon tax puts on families, especially in the cost of filling up the family car, she waved it off as no biggie. People could just do without, if need be. Said Notley, "it's not just a question of having a more fuel-efficient vehicle, it could sometimes be a question of taking a bus, walking, you know, those kinds of things in terms of the patterns of fuel use that people engage in."

(By the way, do you think anyone who describes the way normal families have to haul every day to work, the grocery store, school and soccer practice as "the patterns of fuel use that people engage in" has any actual idea of how real people have to get by in the real world?)

Well, if the NDP knows what's "better" for us regular folks, then at least Albertans can be confident that Notley's climate-obsessed socialists are leading by example, because after all, the very planet is supposed to be at stake or something. Just listen to the fiery and inspiring words of Shannon Phillips, environment minister, in her keynote address at a 2015 Edmonton climate summit. "There is a great appetite for action on climate change in our province, and the days of denial are over," Phillips said at the gathering organized by the Pembina Institute. "Credibility doesn't come from pie-in-the-sky commitments. It comes from saying you are going to do something and then actually doing it."

Yeah, about that credibility... On a particularly frosty winter day the following year, appearing on CBC radio, the interviewer might have had her powerful call to action still ringing in his ears when he asked her how she made her way to the studios that day. Did she take the tremendous opportunity of a cold day outside to make better choice to demonstrate her appetite for action on climate change with credibility?

Of course not. Don't be silly.

Phillips admitted that she drove in that day. And that she routinely flies from her riding in Lethbridge to work in Edmonton. But fighting climate change "isn't about one person's commute," she said. Meaning it's not about *her* commute. It's about *your* commute, as Notley said, and you "taking a bus (or) walking." Maybe Shannon Phillips might even wave from the warmth of her government SUV as her driver speeds past your bus stop.

That's not an exaggeration, by the way. The NDP actually has a thing for big cars. In the first nine months of 2016, NDP cabinet ministers and their deputies expensed $1.47 million for vehicle costs. But they weren't touring Wildrose country in a fleet of electric-powered Nissan Leafs or even hybrid Priuses. Those aren't comfortable. Those are the kinds of better choices the government is trying to tax you into making by making you pay more for gas, but these people have expense accounts (also paid by your taxes), so they can ride in some style. So they arranged for two Nissan Murano crossover SUVs, a Volvo XC60 SUV, two Infiniti JX 35 luxury SUVs, a GMC Acadia AWD SUV, and a Jeep Grand Cherokee SUV.

You would think that kind of hypocrisy would burn just a little; that the NDP's luxury-SUV-driving climate warriors would at least come up with some reason why they needed to be jaunting around in a bunch of hulking gas-slurpers. Maybe for security reasons? Do their aides need all the extra cargo space for their files or something? But no. When someone asked Service Alberta Minister Stephanie Maclean why the government wasn't making better choices to stave off the impending doom of climate change that they're so sure we need to sacrifice ourselves for, she defended the sturdy ride as necessary for handling Alberta's sometimes volatile weather conditions.

"As somebody who spends six hours a week on the QE2, and does that in treacherous road conditions, I need to have a vehicle that is appropriate for the driving conditions," she said. "Any minister and deputy minister needs to have a vehicle that is safe and can contend with the treacherous road conditions that we have in the winter."

Well, yeah, obviously. And six hours commuting a week isn't even that much, compared to what some families have to drive every week between schools, work, after-school stuff and running errands. Sometimes they even have to do it in treacherous road conditions. And they need a vehicle that is safe, too. And they're chauffeuring around people far more important than just a regular old government minister: They're driving kids!

But think about that. Ministers think they're more important. They think their safety matters, when the roads are bad, but not yours. They actually want to tax you into a smaller more dangerous car, while they swan around in their fat, all-wheel-drive SUVs. Could they be more elitist? Could they be more transparent about their lack of concern for the very real challenges faced every day by regular Albertan families?

Well, as a matter of fact, they could be even more elitist and contemptuous. They could literally shout insults at Albertans with whom they disagree.

And that's exactly what they've been doing. In 2016, at the Alberta NDP convention, a year after they had taken power, the mood was understandably celebratory. But things quickly turned nasty, as they have a habit of doing when Notley and the NDP are gloating about how much better they are than the rest of us. Notley tore into those who dared oppose her party's plan, saying "our government caucus looked the anger machine in the eye and said. 'this is one government you are not going to shout down.'"

"The anger machine"? Who did she mean? The opposition parties — as in, the ones supported by the 60 per cent of Albertans who did not vote NDP in the 2015 election? Or did she mean the actual Albertans themselves who don't support her policies? The farmers who had been rallying against her attacks attempting to unionize their home businesses? It could well be: Her MLA Shaye Anderson had called one peaceful rally against her farm attacks "extremely violent and brutal." It wasn't.

But those are the sorts of smears that the NDP so casually throws around about anyone in Albertan who isn't one of them. They're violent. They're angry. They're brutal. They're "sewer rats."

Seriously — that's what the deputy premier actually called some Albertans: "sewer rats." It was in the Legislature. Deputy Premier Sarah Hoffman said of the opposition Wildrose party, "They're spending a lot of time with sewer rats." So that's what she thinks of the Wildrose, or today's Conservatives, or just people who disagree with her.

It was like Hillary Clinton's "basket of deplorables" moment. It revealed in just a few words the scorn that the NDP holds for conservative Albertans. It's why they've been embarrassed for so long about this province: Because it was being run by people who are different. To Notley's NDP, people who think differently than them are gross, like rats. They're fools who need to be punished with taxes for their wrong choices. The NDP is embarrassed by people who don't believe in their radical, socialist, big-labour, big government, anti-oil, climate-crazy agenda. In other words, most Albertans.

CHAPTER 4

TRUDEAU'S WILLING PARTNER

Rachel Notley wants you to know she's standing up. Her government is "standing up for Alberta's energy sector and fighting for Alberta's future," she tweeted in September 2018. When the Alberta's teachers union held a conference in 2018 and invited Notley's former adviser and the longtime anti-oilsands campaigner Tzeporah Berman to bash oil, pipelines and Alberta, Notley followed with a speech to "counter" Berman, with Notley claiming she was "standing up for Alberta." Last December she tweeted that she said she was "proud (to) #StandUp4HumanRights… for workers… & a living wage" and also she was proud to "stand up, every day, to protect the rights of LGBTQ2S+." She said she was also "standing up for Cold Lake." Last September, she said she was going to Ottawa to "stand up for Alberta's energy sector." In August she said she was committed to "standing up for working people and our environment." Last May, she said she was "standing up for Alberta fire fighters." That same month, she said she was "standing up for women." In April, she said she was "standing up" for the Trans Mountain pipeline expansion.

That's a lot of standing up. But the thing about standing up for things is you generally don't have to continue to loudly tell people you're standing up for things. You'd think it would be obvious, without having to come out and repeat it over and over and over again. After all, most people would normally assume that an Alberta premier would stand up for Alberta, without the premier having to constantly assure them that she is. But then, Notley's not your typical premier. She spent her entire career before becoming premier dedicated to not standing up for so many things that are important to Albertans — the oilsands, pipelines, workers, jobs, the energy sector — that it's hard for anyone to believe she would now. And even since she became premier, the evidence keeps mounting around her government that they don't really believe in standing up for those things, even now.

She stands against us.

Notley already didn't support the Northern Gateway pipeline, aligning herself with the Trudeau Liberals' climate crusade, saying the proposal for the pipeline to the northern coast of B.C. was "not the right decision" and that "There's too much environmental sensitivity there and there's genuine concern by the Indigenous communities." Her environment minister, Shannon Phillips, before she was elected even showed up to the National Energy Board hearings to argue against Northern Gateway's approval.

But when Quebec began to push back on the Energy East pipeline, using highly exaggerated claims about environmental damage to block Alberta's oil, Notley supported them. She told the French-language magazine *L'Actualité* that Quebec was entitled to conduct "environmental studies and thoroughly analyze the project to make sure it is safe. I would do the same if an oil pipeline was going to cross my backyard, so I understand".

She considered it necessary for Quebec to ensure the Energy East pipeline was "safe"?

Does she think Alberta oil, which is shipped every day through the existing first-generation Trans Mountain pipeline to Burnaby, B.C.

and through numerous pipelines down to the Gulf Coast, suddenly isn't safe?

And she'd want to be careful if they were in her "backyard?" There are already numerous pipelines in Alberta, in Notley's "backyard." They're safe. They have a far better safety record than any shipping alternative.

In 2016, Notley's deputy premier, Sarah Hoffman, told *Le Devoir* that she thought Quebec's concerns about Energy East were "reasonable."

So much for Notley standing up for pipelines.

In fact, far from "standing up" for them, Notley has literally gone along with every single anti-pipeline and anti-oil policy that the Trudeau Liberals have come up with.

When they wanted to cancel Northern Gateway, she did too.

The Liberals surrendered to Quebec's fight against Energy East. So Notley did, too.

And like the federal Liberals, Notley says pipelines need to be acceptable to the "national interest," not just because Alberta has a right to export its products. After she helped the Liberals narrow down the pipeline to just one out of three options, she bragged in the legislature about how it was all because her government had gone out of its way to accommodate "national interests": "We have gotten a pipeline approved — construction is scheduled to start this fall — and that happened because our government is working hard on addressing and accommodating national interests, including those with respect to climate change, because that is the way you lead." Of course, the construction didn't start. The pipeline is no longer approved. And there's not nearly as much "national interest" about Alberta coming from B.C., Quebec and other opponents compared to the interest Notley seems to have in them.

Is that really how you lead?

And of course when the federal Liberals came up with their carbon-taxing "Pan-Canadian Framework on Clean Growth and Climate Change" Notley was first in line to sign up. "We'll be a willing partner," she said in 2016 — before adding "but we need a willing partner in Ottawa who is going to stand up for Alberta when we have needs, which we do." You would expect an Alberta premier wouldn't agree right off the bat to be a "willing partner" to Ottawa first — and then ask if perhaps Ottawa might consider doing the same. Pretty please? Notley was already pro-carbon-tax, of course, and had slapped one on Alberta long before Trudeau demanded it (she claimed it would get us "social licence" for our pipelines, remember?). But once Trudeau decided it needed to be even higher, the Notley government got itself ready to jump and said "how high"? As Environment Minister Shannon Phillips explained after Trudeau announced his plan, "our carbon price increases will track with the federal legislation." Again, nothing asked in return. Whatever Justin wants, Justin gets ... from the Alberta NDP.

What would it take for the NDP to "stand up" for Alberta's interests against Trudeau, or B.C., or anyone?

Other premiers, outside Alberta, have actually been willing to do more to stand up for our interests than Notley has. It's outrageous. As the Trudeau government has tried to push through Bill C-69, one of the most dangerous pieces of legislation ever to threaten Alberta's economic future, Notley has refused to stand with other premiers in opposition. At the August 2018 Energy and Mines Ministers' Conference in Iqaluit, which included the federal minister and all the provincial ministers, federal Liberal natural resource minister Amarjeet Sohi tried getting the provinces to back a communiqué supporting his government's ruinous Bill C-69, the so-called Impact Assessment Act. The ministers from Saskatchewan and Ontario rightly refused. Instead they issued their own statement properly calling out Bill C-69 as the terrible and job-killing legislation that it is. "The changes in the new Impact Assessment Act would result in a more complex, costly and time-consuming process, while creating uncertainty that could ultimately erode Canada's economic competitiveness," they wrote.

But guess who was happy to back the Liberals instead? That's right: Notley's energy minister, Margaret McCuaig-Boyd. She didn't object one bit. And so Alberta signed right on the communiqué, siding with Sohi to back the federal government's plan to "ensure an effective regulatory review process that enhances economic competitiveness and maintains a sustainable environment."

Except Bill C-69 does nothing of the sort. Canada already had an "effective regulatory review process" with the National Energy Board (NEB), which had been working just fine in reviewing major energy projects until Trudeau's government decided to tear the whole thing down to create a "progressive" regulator focused on global climate change and gender issues rather than Canada's economic interests. The NEB was "widely admired internationally" for its excellent regulatory policies and record, as the *Financial Post's* Claudia Cattaneo noted after the Trudeau government announced it was going to destroy it. Its "technical and administrative competency was admired around the world," was how Gwyn Morgan, the founding CEO of energy giant Encana described it, too.

But Trudeau, a trust-fund baby and part-time drama teacher turned politician, who has never worked in business and has no actual economic training, thinks he knows better about how energy projects should be managed.

Trudeau had his own priorities in deciding to destroy the NEB and replace it with his Bill C-69 plan to pander to the anti-oil, climate-crusading far left. And so he set about trashing the otherwise excellent reputation of the NEB. He said he would "put some teeth" into what he called a "gutted" regulatory review process. He would "restore robust oversight" that he claimed was missing from the NEB reviews, and "ensure that decisions are based on science, facts, and evidence, and serve the public's interest." As if the NEB were making decisions based on superstition and rumour, all while apparently working against the public interest by sometimes actually approving energy projects, and all the jobs and investment that come with them.

That's why business leaders and experts in the energy industry are calling C-69 the "no more pipelines" bill. Trudeau has designed it to ensure that nothing gets approved, ever. When he said he would replace the NEB with a regulator focused on "science, facts and evidence" and serving the "public interest," he actually meant the opposite. His government's Bill C-69 will instead consider "climate impacts," which are based on theories, even if those theories are widely accepted by a lot of scientists, but not actually facts and evidence. He wants pipelines and other projects considered based on "traditional knowledge of Indigenous people" and "views of the public," neither of which, by definition, has anything do with science, facts and evidence.

Bill C-69 also makes it so that anyone can testify at regulatory hearings, even if they're not directly affected by an energy project. Think about that. Under the old process, every single Alberta pipeline project was already plagued with endless delays as a parade of opponents who actually were connected somehow to the proposal — First Nations along the proposed route, or environmental groups complaining about the affected habitat — deliberately frustrated and dragged down the process. It was their strategy: Death by a thousand cuts. Now Trudeau's bill will invite anyone who wants to weigh in to have a voice in the hearings. They don't even need to be affected by the project. It turns a process that doomed projects to death by a thousand cuts into death by a million cuts.

Weirdest of all, C-69's "impact assessment" mandate requires regulators to weigh energy projects based on "the intersection of sex and gender with other identity factors." What does that even mean? Even anti-oilsands environmentalists can't figure that one out. Trudeau's anti-pipeline stance is so radical, it's apparently beyond anything even anti-oilsands radicals understand. "If you're asking, 'What does that mean?' I'm going to have to say I don't really know," Richard Lindgren, a staff lawyer at the Canadian Environmental Law Association, told the *National Post.* Gender and identity intersectionality is the kind of neo-Marxist social justice theory they teach in Women's Studies and Queer Studies courses at second-rate liberal arts colleges. It is the polar opposite of science, facts and evidence. It is literally stuff people have made up.

But that's the point. Trudeau wants to make it possible to kill energy projects by any means necessary. If he can't find environmental excuses to do it, or "traditional" aboriginal knowledge to do it, he'll use sophomoric gender-studies gobbledygook to do it. Because that's exactly what a clause like this can do, according to an analysis by the law firm Osler, Hoskin and Harcourt LLP: it makes decisions political, rather than scientific and based on technical expertise. It makes "the role of an impact assessment more of a policy-setting exercise than focused on the merits of a specific project," concludes Osler. And the result is "likely to increase the scope of studies the proponents will need to engage in and contribute to overall project uncertainty." In other words, more hurdles, more red tape and fewer projects being built. And by fewer, you can be sure that means none.

TransCanada spent roughly $1 billion trying to get Energy East approved, until Trudeau decided to throw upstream and downstream climate considerations into the process as a way of successfully getting the company to abandon the project — as in, the pipeline would be judged by how people might make or use the oil that was put through it — a bizarre test no other oil is subjected to, especially Canadian oil imports, including from OPEC.

Under C-69, what investor would be foolish enough to wager hundreds of millions of dollars just to put together a proposal when it can all be undone not just by the same ever-shifting climate goalposts, but also by public protests, First Nations anecdotes and an indefinable and therefore perennially unattainable demand to incorporate gender and identity theories?

As if it wasn't already difficult enough getting projects approved, after Energy East, Northern Gateway and even Trans Mountain got snarled up in politics, court rulings, First Nations opposition and political problems so that none of them have been able to proceed after years and years of trying. Enbridge estimates that C-69 will nearly double the approval timeline for a pipeline. Canadian Energy Pipeline Association president Chris Bloomer told the House of Commons' environment committee: "It is difficult to imagine that a new major pipeline could be built under the Impact Assessment Act (Bill C-69), much less attract energy investment to Canada." Even Cameco, the Saskatchewan Uranium mining giant, concluded that C-69's "proposed assessment processes are wholly impractical and illogical and, in our view, will never result in a major project approval."

So why isn't the Alberta government fighting this bill with everything it's got? After all, there are senators in Ottawa who certainly are. Alberta

Senator Doug Black, who sits as an Independent, has been fighting to block the bill in the Senate. He sees the bill as part of the plan already underway to kill the oilsands, being pursued by climate extremists in the federal government, no doubt including the prime minister's top adviser, Gerald Butts (who recently resigned in the wake of the scandal over interference with the justice system to protect a Quebec company, SNC-Lavalin). "I believe there are parts of the government that believe that would be a desirable outcome," Black has said. Even Nova Scotia Senator Michael MacDonald recognizes the potential destruction that C-69 could cause and is doing his best to prevent it. "Many informed people consider Bill C-69 to be a reckless piece of legislation that will cripple resource development in Canada, and exacerbate the deteriorating employment situation in these industries," MacDonald recently wrote in an op-ed in the *National Post.*

And what about Rachel Notley? Has she written any op-eds to expose the dangers of C-69 and to call on Canadians to stop it? Has she sounded the alarm about how this will end any future hope for energy projects in Alberta? Has she loudly and forcefully demanded that the Trudeau government abandon it?

Of course not.

On the contrary, Notley not only had her minister sign on to the Liberal government's communiqué backing C-69, refusing to join Saskatchewan and Ontario in boycotting the gesture. She has actually been helping the Liberals all along with C-69. In March 2018, Alberta Opposition leader Jason Kenney, of the United Conservative Party, wrote a friendly letter to Notley saying that both parties needed to team up and work together to stop C-69. "Before this legislation is pushed through, it is imperative that we make clear to all involved that Albertans stand united against these changes," Kenney wrote. He asked her to consider uniting together to back a motion in the Alberta legislature: "Be it resolved that the Legislative Assembly stand(s) opposed to the Government of Canada's proposed Impact Assessment Act that will further diminish investor confidence in Alberta's energy industry, jeopardizing Alberta jobs." Kenney even told Notley was "open to modifying this draft language in an effort to find all-party consensus on this issue that is so critical to our economic future" and guaranteed Notley the "assurance of my full cooperation to do what we can to unite the Legislative Assembly in speaking for Albertans on this issue."

Speak for Albertans? Not Notley. She ignored the letter. And then, when Kenney tabled the motion in the legislature, she had her government vote against it.

Notley's environment minister in April refused even to say that the government opposed C-69 when she was asked directly about it. Notley's energy minister, Margaret McCuaig-Boyd even mocked Kenney and his party's deep concern over the damage that C-69 would cause. "I am somewhat puzzled why you guys are so obsessed with the federal government and what they're doing. Maybe that's where you need to be instead of across the way," McCuaig-Boyd said in the Legislature in April.

No wonder Notley's government wouldn't come out and publicly oppose C-69. Just a month after the Saskatchewan and Ontario governments took a public stand against it at the ministers conference in Iqaluit, Notley was readily giving credit to the Trudeau government for heading in the right direction with the bill. In an interview with *BNN Bloomberg*, Notley "said she agrees with the goals of Ottawa's new environmental impact legislation," and her only concerns were that it needed to tighten up the details. "It's just that we are spending a lot of time going back and forth with (Ottawa) on the details and we are not yet at the point where we are finding details that have been resolved," she said. So it's not detailed enough? So that's her problem with a bill that will double the timeline for the already convoluted approval process and will test the viability of Alberta energy projects against the professionally organized opposition of billion-dollar American anti-oilsands foundations, stories passed down from Aboriginal elders and the opinions of transgender studies professors?

Apparently so. She has said she thinks C-69 has a "good intent." Around the same time she was telling *BNN Bloomberg* she "agrees with the goals" of Trudeau's pipeline-killing bill, she gathered reporters to offer even more supportive comments to the plan. "Notley told reporters she has no quibbles with the goal of C-69: to create a regulatory regime that Canadians trust," the *Canadian Press* reported. "I support their intent, but you need to really engage really carefully to make sure that you don't kill yourself with good intentions." Right. All those "good intentions" that the Trudeau government has for Alberta's oil industry are the problem. That's what's led to tens of thousands of job losses, investors turning their back on Alberta and companies fleeing the oilpatch. Blame it on Trudeau's good intentions.

And it hasn't been just on C-69 where Notley and her government have sounded more like they're standing up for Alberta's enemies than they are standing up for Alberta. In 2018, the Trudeau government informed the Notley government that it planned to renew the existing equalization formula, ensuring that Alberta would keep paying more than any other province, despite the province having endured half a decade of some of the hardest times its ever seen, and guaranteeing Quebec a bonus handout of $1.4 billion, increasing Quebec's take to $13 billion in free money, with Alberta families shouldering the heaviest cost for that giveaway.

What did Notley's finance minister, Joe Ceci, do when he got the letter from his federal counterpart, Finance Minister Bill Morneau, that the Liberals in Ottawa were planning to screw Alberta on equalization?

Nothing.

Morneau notified Ceci of his plan to renew the vastly unfair equalization program in May. And Ceci did nothing. He didn't challenge Morneau. He didn't even ask him for a meeting to change his mind. He didn't go public and warn Albertans this was about to happen, thus preventing any public outcry, and making it impossible for Alberta's MPs and Senators in Ottawa to fight it. Ceci simply did nothing. He sat back and let it happen.

The rest of Alberta wouldn't find out until June that, with no response from Alberta, the Trudeau government had gone ahead and officially renewed the equalization formula, setting yet another rip-off for Alberta in stone for another six years, until it comes up for renewal again in 2024. A sentence of six years of financial punishment for Albertans. When reporters asked Ceci why he didn't do something when he had the chance and fight Ottawa to stop it, all he could offer was "I don't think that's the right decision."

The thing is, Notley's NDP apparently never thinks it's the "right decision" to stand up for Alberta to Ottawa, or to anyone else. Just a few months after the NDP took power in 2015, Ceci had already tipped his hand that he had no plans to fight for Alberta on the equalization file. Ceci told *The Globe and Mail* that "he gets phone calls and letters from residents asking why the province still contributes to equalization when it is experiencing negative economic growth," but admitted he wasn't about to do anything about it. "However, he said he has no plans to lobby Ottawa for changes because there would be little sympathy."

Wait... sympathy? Is that what he expects? That's how he thinks change happens? Because people are sympathetic to Alberta? Has Alberta ever gotten sympathy from the Liberals in Ottawa? Or Quebec? Or most anywhere in Canada for that matter? Sympathy for Alberta and a dollar won't even buy you a decent cup of coffee in this country. Alberta has never had its demands met because of sympathy; Alberta has only had its demands met when its government actually stands up for Albertans. When it fights. When it uses its economic clout and its energy power to make Ottawa listen.

But just a couple of months after Ceci told the *Globe* that he "had no plans" to fight the equalization attacks on Alberta, he was again dismissing demands by the then Opposition leader, Brian Jean, to stand up for Alberta and do something about equalization. No thanks, said Ceci. That "won't make a whit of difference for Albertans today," Ceci told the *Calgary Herald* in February 2016. And, according to that *Herald* report, Ceci said that "Equalization won't be on the Notley government's agenda until closer to 2019."

Oh, 2019? As in, the year after the federal Liberals had already renewed the existing scheme. A year after Ceci could have actually done anything about it. A year after the swindle against Alberta was officially re-established for another six years. That's when equalization will finally be on the Notley government's agenda.

When you look at how the NDP at every turn has not only not stood up for Alberta, but has actually given tacit support to pipeline opponents, equalization schemes and job-killing regulatory overhauls, you have to wonder who the NDP is really standing up for. When Opposition leader Jason Kenney said Alberta should stand up to the B.C. NDP government and impose provincial trade sanctions over its attempts to block the Trans Mountain expansion, Notley mocked him. "He's essentially saying that, what we should do is build a wall around Alberta," she told *CTV News*. "I wouldn't be surprised if, tomorrow, he comes out demanding that B.C. pays for it." Har har. Get it?

And she mocked Kenney's fight against Ottawa's carbon tax. "It doesn't help anyone. It just undermines our credibility," she told the *Calgary Sun's* Rick Bell in December 2017. Except, nine months later, Notley would have to publicly admit that Ottawa had screwed Alberta on the carbon tax, by not delivering any pipelines in return, and said she would no longer agree to match the federal government's planned increases. But then, Notley's carbon tax is already so much higher than the federal one, her carbon tax won't be out of line with the federal one until 2021, anyway. She isn't even willing to cancel the carbon tax now as a way of fighting Ottawa to get better treatment for our pipelines and energy industry. Maybe she might do something about it in a few years. Maybe.

But even if Notley were still around and a carbon tax is still around in 2021, why would anyone believe she would actually make good on her promise to take even that feeble a stand? Time and time again, Notley has had the chance to get tough and stand up for Alberta — and she's backed down. Remember in February 2018 when she invoked a ban on imports to Alberta of B.C. wine supposedly to get the government in Victoria to back off its opposition to Alberta pipelines? That barely lasted two weeks. Notley revoked it the first chance she got. B.C. had been planning to put a limit on any more Alberta bitumen coming into the province by rail or pipeline, as part of its fight against pipelines and everything else related to Alberta oil. B.C.'s NDP government is still pursuing that — B.C.'s NDP Premier John Horgan hasn't backed down on his side — but he did refer the plan to a court for a review of its legality. That was enough for Notley. B.C. wine was back in business in Alberta, even if Alberta's oil was still stuck trying to get past B.C.

And remember in May 2018 when Notley's NDP actually passed a bill giving it the power to choke off oil and gas exports to B.C.? What was that for, exactly? Notley never used it. She never will. B.C. depends heavily on Alberta's energy exports, even as its government constantly works to sabotage our exports. Cutting off oil and gas would hit B.C. where it hurts. A lot more than wine. But Notley's NDP doesn't really want to punish B.C.'s NDP, even as the B.C. government continues to harm our province. Notley doesn't really want to stand up for Alberta.

She never did.

CHAPTER 5

SOCIALIST SABOTAGE

Rachel Notley's NDP didn't just set out to fight Alberta's businesses and key industries. They set out to change Alberta, permanently, from a freedom-loving, pro-business, capitalist province to a beachhead for the NDP's globalist socialist vision for Canada. Notley may be temporarily on the outs with some of her fellow NDP leaders, including John Horgan in B.C. and federal leader Jagmeet Singh, because she had to soften her anti-pipeline views once she was elected premier of Alberta. But long before their family squabble began over pipelines, the NDP has always stood for socialism, whether it's in B.C., in Alberta or in Ottawa. Rachel Notley has long been a warrior for the anti-capitalist left. And one of her top priorities even after she was elected was to figure out a way to permanently change the direction of this province from a pro-business province to a big government province. On that front, she's made great strides.

How did she do it? As more and more Albertans lost their jobs from the private sector over the last four years, thanks to a deadly combination of her carbon taxes, new corporate taxes, royalty uncertainty and oilsands restrictions, Notley made sure to keep growing the size of the union-dominated public sector. The NDP has spent the last four years touting what it calls its "jobs plan," while failing to note that its plan is for taxpayer-funded jobs for public sector workers. That is, jobs that don't create income, but rather, jobs that take your income.

The Notley NDP took power in 2015, the year after oil prices started to collapse. Since that downturn, however, despite falling commodity prices, shrinking revenues and massive layoffs in the private sector, the NDP ballooned the public sector, increasing jobs paid for by taxpayers by an astounding 21.5 per cent. As of early 2018, that added up to more than 78,000 more jobs in the public sector, according to the Fraser Institute's analysis of Statistics Canada figures, while the total number of private sector jobs fell by more than 46,000 jobs over the same period, and private sector employment overall fell by three per cent. The result, says the Fraser Institute, is that "the primary driver of total employment growth (in Alberta) is an increase in government sector employment." Saskatchewan experienced the same commodity downturn but even there, where Prairie socialism is part of the provincial fabric, government jobs only grew one-tenth of what they did over the same period under Notley's NDP. In 2014, just one in five Albertans worked in a government job at one level or another. Twenty years ago, it was one in six. In just four short years, the NDP made it so that now one in four — fully 25 per cent — of workers in the province are part of the government. Talk about socialism in a hurry.

Notley knows that even if she can't get re-elected again, she can tie the hands of future leaders by swelling the government to such a size that it would take deep cuts to get it back down again — the very thing she is now warning that the United Conservative Party will want to do if it gets elected, as she tries scaring Albertans away from her rivals. UCP leader Jason Kenney will deploy "reckless cuts," she warned recently, "Cuts of billions of dollars for things people need," she said. But of course, Albertans don't "need" 80,000 more government workers than they had four years ago. Albertans don't "need" tens of thousands more public-sector union jobs taking their taxes away. What Albertans "need" are private sector jobs, the jobs that create wealth, not jobs that take away wealth.

But Notley's made sure that isn't going to happen. As she vastly expanded the public sector, she did everything she could to starve the private sector of investment that would create those wealth-producing jobs.

It's hard to overstate just how ruinous her high-tax, heavy-regulation, anti-carbon, anti-employer campaign has been, but it may rank as one of the most successful destructions of economic strength since Hugo Chavez's Bolivarian Revolution in Venezuela — which, hard as it is to believe, was actually held up as a model for Alberta to follow by people inside Notley's NDP.

Around the world, the oil business has been on a tear. Inside Notley's Alberta, the oil business has suffocated. Last fall, oil analysts at Wood Mackenzie Ltd. projected that international energy firms would be rolling out US$300 billion in new investment around the world in the next couple of years. Now, almost none of that will be coming to what was once the most stable, friendly jurisdiction for oil and gas on the planet. In fact, Statistics Canada reports that Canada has lost at least $60 billion in energy investment since 2015.

Is anyone surprised? Sure, some of the blame for that lies with the federal Liberals, who have done their own part to cripple Alberta's energy industry. But no premier in the province has stood by Prime Minister Justin Trudeau's destructive anti-oil climate policies more solidly than Notley has. That's because she started hammering Alberta's oil sector even before Trudeau did. She barely waited a month after being elected to announce a major review of Alberta's royalty take, even though the industry was at the time already suffering the worst of the oil-price collapse. For five months, while her handpicked advisers, headed by self-described environmental warrior Dave Mowat, investment in the oil and gas industry in Alberta was virtually paralyzed as it waited to see the new economics of oil and gas in the province. And it turns out it was completely unnecessary. Even Mowat and his panel had to concede that the royalties really didn't need reviewing, after all: the Alberta government had been getting its "fair share" all along. But by putting that fright into investors virtually the moment she was elected, Notley set the tone for what would be four very bleak years for Alberta investment.

That was just the start for what would be a series of policies that couldn't have been better designed at discouraging oil and gas companies, and pretty much any other business, from setting up shop in Alberta. In their first budget, they increased the burden of Alberta's corporate tax rate by a full 20 per cent, raising it from 10 points to 12, taking Alberta from having the most competitive business environment in the country, with the lowest taxes, to the same as other provinces. They increased taxes on high-skilled high earners — the sort of people needed to run the energy sector — by a full 50 per cent, from 10 points to 15 points.

Notley didn't stop there. Then she announced a sweeping and draconian "climate plan" that would strangle whatever life was left in Alberta's already suffering oil and gas industry. And she appointed as advisers to her climate policy plan none other than some of the most vehemently anti-oilsands, anti-Albertan eco-activists in Canada today: Tzeporah Berman, Tim Gray, Alison Ronson and Karen Mahon. And of course they delivered a plan to literally punish Alberta's oil industry with carbon taxes and restrictions on further expansion.

What else would you expect after Notley appointed a team of anti-oil zealots to decide the future of Alberta's oil industry? Berman leads the war against the oilsands and pipelines and compares Alberta's oilsands to the fictional hellscape of "Mordor" in *The Lord of the Rings* trilogy. She is probably one of the biggest, if not the biggest enemies of Alberta oil in the entire country. And she doesn't care who knows it. Then there's Tim Gray, executive director of Environmental Defence, one of the most powerful lobby groups working to kill Alberta's oilsands. Ronson, as a director of the Canadian Parks and Wilderness Society, was helping run a group that has opposed pipelines from Alberta. And Mahon is the national director of the extremist group Stand.earth, and has vowed that the Trans Mountain pipeline "will never be built" and to fight it "in the streets" and in the "forest." She was even arrested trying to block a Kinder Morgan ship in a protest by kayak. Could Notley have even found any worse enemies of Alberta oil to appoint to a panel to draft new rules for Alberta oil? Probably not. Could Notley have waved a bigger red flag for investors to stay the hell away from Alberta? Not a chance.

Socialists aren't big fans of the private sector. Their modus operandi is to nationalize whatever they can, to make it another government service, employing more public servants, taking more taxpayer money, while destroying private enterprise and wealth. That's not easy to do in Alberta, where people have faith in the market, and where, thanks to Ralph Klein's privatization binge, we've seen everything from liquor retailing to registries run better, more efficiently, and cheaper than when it was all under government control.

But the NDP has doing its best to take us backwards — back to the days of bad service provided by overpaid and unmotivated unionized government employees. When Alberta Health Services tried outsourcing its laundry service to a private company, the NDP wouldn't have it. They literally nationalized the service.

They nationalized the laundry.

Does that even make sense to anyone? Laundry is something everyone does. There are dozens and dozens of private companies that provide good laundry service to retirement homes, restaurants, private clinics, you name it. It's one of the easiest things to outsource. And it's so much cheaper to do it than to have the government own laundry services. Really, have you even heard of a government doing laundry before? And heaven knows if there's one area where Alberta could stand to save some money, it's the health system, where more money freed up for patients, to lower the long waits at ER and for surgeries, would be so much better spent than on expensive public-sector union employees and administrators all hired to manage something as basic as washing towels and sheets.

Even Dr. David Swann, the former leader of the Alberta Liberals, who was often in favour of bigger government himself, called the decision absurd. "This ministerial intervention was based on ideology, rather than a solid business case," Swann said in a news release. "We now know this plan is not going to save jobs or money. The millions of dollars required for AHS to do its own laundry could be better spent on patient care, salaries and critical infrastructure."

But that was just the start. The NDP's next nationalization was aimed at taking Alberta's driver's license testing back out of the private market — where it had been working fine for more than 25 years. And yet again, it was a terrible decision made for ideological reasons that only ended up causing more problems.

In an NDP press release at the time, Transportation Minister Brian Mason said the current framework has limited oversight and is vulnerable to many problems such as inconsistent fees for service and reduced access in rural areas and an overall lack of integrity.

That's a pretty serious allegation against the 153 independent privatized road-test providers in the province — accusing private-sector Albertans of lacking integrity. As if the NDP government has so much of it.

Even if these issues were happening, this is certainly something that could be addressed through standardized regulations rather than having the state literally seize the sector and take it over for itself.

Industry organizations representing the examiners said the government refused to meet with them to even discuss fair market compensation before this Venezuelan-style seizure took place in March 2019.

And so, not surprisingly, as soon as the province went public with its plans, and its smear against private operators, people who provide driver's licence examinations began walking off the job and abandoning the small businesses they had built from the ground up.

Not only is it atrocious to think that the NDP government would first steal your successful business from you because they think they can do it better than you, and then refuse to give you at least fair market value for the business they stole, but I think the worst part of all of this is this is all just based on another NDP lie and their own numbers prove it.

And it's all there in the NDP press release where they first announced this government takeover of private enterprise. Here's what it said:

- On average, Alberta Transportation receives seven complaints about driver examinations every weekday.
- More than 200,000 road tests for all driver's license classes were conducted in Alberta in 2016.

Hmm. Seven complaints a day. That might sound a lot, but let's do the math to find out. Seven a day, times five government business days a year, times 52 weeks a year: That's 1,820 complaints per year across the entire province.

But the government revealed that in 2016 there were more than 200,000 road tests for all driver-licence classes.

That's less than a one-per-cent complaint rate. And how many of those complaints are legitimate anyway? What if even half of these complaints are just people upset because they failed their tests — people who think they should have passed because they think they know how to drive but really don't?

This tiny, fraction of a per cent complaining out of hundreds of thousands of tests overall is what the NDP claims justifies the nationalization of an entire industry? Talk about ideological garbage.

The NDP isn't just making up a fake problem. It's making up a fake problem so it can steal the business and livelihoods of hard-working driving testers, while smearing their reputations for integrity. As usual, the NDP can't govern honestly. It can only do it through lies and reputational destruction.

But Notley's nationalization hasn't stopped there; she's literally seized part of the oil and gas sector, too. As if this were the days of the National Energy Program. Or Venezuela.

In December 2018, Notley decided she would order oil companies to stop producing oil, as a way of propping up prices, because there was a glut that was causing a discount, and that was hurting government revenues. But ordering production cuts to raise prices is how the autocrats at OPEC do things. Not Alberta.

To be fair, the decidedly un-conservative idea to have Alberta's overwhelmingly inept left-wing government intervene to cut production of oil came from an unlikely source: United Conservative Party leader Jason Kenney.

But if he meant it for real, or to lure Notley into a trap, it sure was an easy sell to the NDP and Notley, who have always wanted control over the production and processing of Alberta's oil. The policy amounted to an embargo on Alberta oil, even while Eastern Canada continued to import hundreds of thousands of barrels of foreign oil every single day.

Notley ran with Kenney's idea and imposed government-mandated production cuts on private companies who had already purchased lease rights to produce oil, free from government intervention. It was an unnecessary move and anti-free-market. Companies can cut production on their own if they decide its unprofitable for them to produce. What Notley was trying to do here was to protect her royalties — she complained loudly that the government was losing tens of millions of dollars of its take every day, due to the discounted prices. And she needed that money to keep up her big-government spending habit. So she did what she needed to maximize government revenues at the expense of thousands of jobs in the upstream extraction side of oil and gas. That's because when you cut production, you're cutting drilling jobs and trucking jobs and all the jobs related to getting the oil out of the ground. Thousands more Albertans were at risk of losing their jobs because of Notley's revenue grab. As if we don't have enough people in this province out of work as it is.

Notley started her embargo in January 2019. In less than a month into the embargo, the Lakeland Connect news outlet in Bonnyville, Alta. was reporting that without changes to Notley's curtailment formula by February 1st, oil company CNRL would be shutting in their assets in Bonneyville, Elk Point and Lloydminster, including the ECHO pipeline which is the main way of getting oil out of the region.

The company estimated that anywhere from 500 to 1,000 direct employees and up to 2,400 contractors and service providers would be out of work in the Lakeland region without a change to the OPEC-style curtailment formula.

By February 1, the government announced that it would be easing the limits on production for February and March for CNRL, allowing the company to avoid massive layoffs.

Notley's plan to curtail oil nearly ended a pipeline and risked killing up to 3,400 jobs associated with just one company. Yet when Notley eased the curtailment for CNRL, she laughably claimed this was as a result of the success of her program — instead of the clear and obvious failure and lack of foresight.

But that isn't the only thing curtailment is costing us. Because in addition to taking control of production, Notley also announced in late 2018 that she was taking control of part of the shipping and distribution of Alberta oil, too. The government would actually run its own rail cars to ship oil. In November, Notley told two separate Ontario audiences that the province would be buying roughly 80 locomotives and 7,000 rail cars to meet a goal of shipping an additional 120,000 barrels of oil per day, in lieu of an actual pipeline. She publicly estimated the cost at a third of a billion dollars. Experts estimated that in the end it could end up costing taxpayers more like over $1 billion. Even that turned out to be far too conservative. Notley ended up signing up to spend nearly four times that much: $3.7 billion. But not even to buy the cars, anymore. Now she was just going to lease them. That means $3.7 billion just in rent and expenses. No assets. Just billions of dollars, spent.

But even as Notley was signing taxpayers up to run a government railroad, private sector shippers were actually — get this — cutting back on rail shipping. On Feb. 1, 2019, just a day after Rachel Notley claimed that her curtailment had been such a smashing success, Imperial Oil announced it was cutting its crude-by-rail shipments from 168,000 barrels per day in December to near-zero. And its CEO placed the blame squarely on the Alberta government's oil-production caps. Imperial CEO Rich Krueger said the cuts ruined the economic case for shipping oil by rail to customers in the United States.

As he told investors, "now because of the drastic and dramatic manipulation and impact on differentials, takeaway capacity is now being idled. That is a sad state, a very tangible example of what we believe is an ill-advised, ill-informed, negative consequence of this curtailment order"

Meanwhile, the Financial Post reported that rail volumes fell 56 per cent in the first week of February compared with three weeks earlier and from a high in December — back when the NDP first decided to start meddling in the sector.

So besides continued job losses in upstream production and the evacuation of oilfield investment to smarter, freer jurisdictions that means that Notley's 7,000 new rail cars and 80 new locomotives are basically useless.

On everything from driver testing to laundry to the oil sector, Notley's nationalizations have destroyed wealth and jobs, and made Alberta worse off. Just imagine how much more they'll try nationalizing if they get another four years — and shudder.

CHAPTER 6

KAFKA COMES TO ALBERTA

Rachel Notley and her NDP have acted like thin-skinned bullies from the moment they were elected. Now that they're close to being unelected, they're getting even more thuggish.

They're actually prosecuting our news organization. The NDP is coming at The Rebel Media using an enforcer who used to work for the Alberta Human Rights Commission. They have given her a special contract to lead the investigation against us. Albertans haven't seen a government try to suppress the media since Bill Aberhardt tried it .... in the 1930s. And even he had his media-muzzling attempts overturned by the courts.

Notley was hoping there isn't time for the legal process to play out. She wanted to shut down The Rebel before the election. Who cares about freedom of the press when there's power to be grabbed? Notley knows we have been their most effective critics, and the NDP will do anything to silence us.

So they unleashed a pre-emptive attack. Notley had the Government of Alberta put us on trial. The charges were that because we criticized Notley, we were more of a political party than a media outlet and so any publicity and advertising we've done — including billboards, like the one we put up in Edmonton criticizing Education Minister Dave Eggen — made us a campaign organization that needed to register with the government.

They didn't even tell us they were putting us on trial. They convicted us in our absence. They let us know afterwards. It's as if Kafka came to Alberta.

We didn't know it, but the commissioner they hired to come after us went ahead and started contacting our vendors, businesses we deal with, and started interfering in our contracts with those businesses, and threatening to come after them if they didn't comply with government orders. That's actually how we found out we'd been charged, tried and convicted. The government didn't tell us; we had to hear it from the Alberta businesses who were threatened by the government, who told us about it.

The day after we were convicted in a secret trial, the day after Notley's hired gun started going after our business partners, we finally received an e-mail from the government of Alberta telling us we had been convicted of being a political campaign organization, not journalists, and that they were looking at fining us $5,500 because our views are apparently not journalistic views, they claim, but rather they are political campaign views and have to be treated as campaign spending.

Except, the law in Alberta is clear: media companies, political commentators, book authors and groups like that are all exempt from political regulation. Here's an excerpt from section 44.1 of the law that was allegedly used against us: "election advertising... does not include the transmutation to the public of an editorial, a debate, a speech, an interview, a column, a letter, a commentary or news." The law also exempts books, and the promotion of books, but let me put down a marker right now: I predict Notley's hand-picked Elections Commissioner will try to prosecute me for the very book you're reading.

The law clearly exempts journalism — including opinion journalism. So, yes, sure, we have opinions at The Rebel. It's my opinion that Rachel

Notley is the worst premier in Alberta history and her government should be fired. But I'm allowed to say that. This is a free country.

The timing of Notley's latest attack on our freedom of the press came right after we put up that billboard criticizing Education Minister David Eggen. It explained that "40% of grade 9 students failed provincial exams" — which is true — and "Alberta can do better than David Eggen." That's also true. So Notley should fire Eggen. That's the kind of opinion that opinion journalists offer all the time, suggesting that it's time for this minister or that minister to step down. Not many Alberta journalists have said anything about getting rid of Notley's terrible cabinet members, so I think she's probably just not used to it. Anyway, David Eggen is the worst education minister in Alberta history. That's an opinion that a lot of Albertans would hold. But Notley wanted to attack us over our opinion.

Now, a $5,500 fine in itself wouldn't bankrupt us. But we're not going to stop our journalism. We're not going to stop our criticism of Notley and her destroyers. We'll keep going to keep doing it. Which means they're going to keep fining us until they succeed in putting us out of business. Or they lose the election. Whichever comes first.

It's important to note that this isn't the first time Notley has tried pulling this. Back in 2017, we received a threat letter from Notley's agents, telling us we were an illegal campaign group. Our lawyer wrote back, explaining the law to Notley's staff — pointing out that we were journalists and therefore exempt under the law. And we didn't hear back from them again. Apparently, they realized they had no leg to stand on.

But then things started to get desperate for Notley. Her government is very much at risk of getting demolished in the next election. Maybe she figured if she waited until just before the election to pull the same trick again, there wouldn't be time for us to fight back before the vote. So on Dec. 17, 2018, we suddenly received a letter from Notley's new campaign enforcer, saying our criticism of Notley's education minister, David Eggen, was illegal, and that we had 14 days to reply. They sent it to us right before Christmas, and demanded a reply on New Year's

Eve. As if anyone in the government bureaucracy would be sitting around waiting for it on New Year's.

So our lawyer, Fred Kozak, wrote to Notley's staff asking if he could reply after Christmas. They agreed. Come January, Kozak wrote again asking for specifics about the complaint against us — what is it exactly that we were supposedly doing illegally. And Notley's people wrote back saying they'd get back to us with that information on January 15th.

But that was actually a hoax. They pulled a fast one. They never did get back to our lawyer on January 15th. In fact, they went ahead and held that secret trial and convicted us and sentenced us on the 14th. And that was entirely illegal. The law says we have the right to reply to accusations. This isn't China. We don't have kangaroo courts here. Except the NDP government does. Rachel Notley, once again, was abusing the law.

She's done that so many times before. She once illegally sent an armed sheriff to personally kick me out the Legislature. That was against the law, and she ended up having to apologize for it.

Then she had the Alberta justice department send us a threatening letter, banning us — or anyone "connected to us," whatever that means — from all government property. Even Toronto newspapers called her a thug for doing that.

Now here Notley goes again, abusing the process for the third time, just to shut down her critics.

In fact, Notley invented the entirely new "Election Commissioner" position just so she could get away with it. An Election Commissioner is different from Elections Alberta, which actually runs the election. This commissioner is less like a watchdog and more of an attack dog, doing dirty work for the NDP. So Notley naturally handpicked an extremely partisan activist to be her Election Commissioner. His name is Lorne Gibson and he hates conservatives — he actually tried suing the former Progressive Conservative government of Alberta for hundreds of thousands of dollars. He was once Alberta's chief electoral officer. He went after the PCs relentlessly and was, as one veteran political columnist called him, "arguably Alberta's most controversial chief electoral officer." And when the PC government let his contract run out with renewing it, he tried suing for wrongful dismissal. But his kooky case was thrown out of court

But when Notley took power, she was looking for a hater with a vendetta against conservatives. She called up Lorne Gibson. And she appointed him over the protests of every single conservative MLA — they all voted against him. Normally neutral, non-partisan people are appointed to these sensitive positions. It's like being a judge. But that's not what Notley wants — she wants a hitman.

And he's done exactly what she wanted. Look at the website of his all-new Election Commission and you'll pretty quickly notice a pattern in who he targets: The Canadian Taxpayers Federation. A Conservative group called Alberta Can't Wait. A pro-life group.

And now he's trying to get The Rebel. No left-wing groups are on his list. No environmental groups. No union groups. None of the NDP front groups, like Press Progress. Just grassroots conservatives.

And what a team Lorne Gibson has helping him out. Remember I said that after The Rebel was convicted in secret, the government started coming after people that do business with us and threatening them? The woman doing that dirty work to help Gibson was a woman named Melanie Malchuk. She worked for years at another kangaroo court: The Alberta Human Rights Commission. That's the place that sued Ezra Levant as the publisher of the *Western Standard* magazine for printing world-famous cartoons from Denmark that dared to represent the Muslim prophet Mohammed. No wonder she's so eager to get back at Levant and The Rebel.

This has all happened in the past few months. Let me be clear: Rachel Notley is coming to kill The Rebel in the run-up to her reelection. We are not going to pay the $5,500 fine. Because it was a kangaroo court, run by out-of-control partisans, who didn't even follow their own law. They didn't show us the complaint, they didn't let us reply, and they're illegally prosecuting journalists. And this time she's got real teeth: if they can abuse the law and turn it against us, they can fine us up to

$100,000 a month. That would bankrupt us. And it would silence one of the few voices in Alberta willing to investigate the lies and abuses of Notley's NDP, and call them out on it. Don't think for a minute that bankrupting us and silencing us is exactly what they want to do.

CHAPTER 7

DRUGS, DALLIANCES AND THE CHIEF OF STAFF

On the eve of the Alberta election campaign The Rebel uncovered shocking news.

Allegations of sexual misconduct against members of her NDP caucus had been dogging Notley's government. And we think we finally got to the bottom of them, despite Notley's attempts to cover the whole thing up and make it quietly go away.

It's a story of misconduct. But just as important, it's a story of how complicit and compliant most of the mainstream media in Alberta is. Just like they all uncritically reported on the fake Value Creation upgrader, without bothering to even check whether construction was indeed "underway", they're all too eager to let ethical lapses by NDP politicians slide. Whether it's out of ideological sympathy, laziness or even the hope of being hired as an NDP spin-doctor, it's an epidemic — Alberta arguably has the most submissive press corps of any province in Canada.

The perfect example of this was the "#MeToo" scandal in Notley's government.

The complaints — which alleged both sexual misconduct and bullying — went as far back as 2015, the year the NDP first took power, but Albertans didn't learn about the accusations against two of Notley's sitting MLAs until November 2018, three years later. And even then, Notley refused to reveal anything about them. She refused to be transparent about who was being accused, what they were accused of doing, who they had allegedly victimized, and what the consequences had been, or even if there were any consequences. All Notley's spokesperson offered was a statement clarifying that "In both circumstances, the alleged behaviour took place outside the workplace" and "In order to respect the privacy of the complainants, further details will remain confidential."

Of course, that wasn't really what was going on. Notley wasn't protecting the privacy of the complainants. It's standard procedure in sexual assault cases to name the accused, but not the victim. That's how police do it when they arrest someone for sexual assault. And if both incidents happened outside the workplace, it hardly follows that naming the MLAs being accused would somehow expose their alleged victims. Notley could have named the alleged perpetrators. She should have named the alleged perpetrators. But she chose to protect them. Party solidarity apparently takes precedence over justice for victims.

Notley wanted to go into the 2019 provincial election with that secret well kept. She didn't want sexual misconduct and bullying scandals ruining her campaign. After all, the NDP want you to think conservatives are the knuckle-dragging, mouth-breathing toxically masculine male chauvinist pigs in this province. Exposing bullies and predators in her caucus would mess with that oh-so-comforting NDP narrative.

In reality, the NDP's internal culture is so toxic that one of their female MLAs, Robyn Luff, felt the need to physically leave the NDP caucus. She refused to sit in the legislature with the other NDP MLAs, explaining in a letter that there was a "culture of fear and intimidation." But rather than taking Luff's complaints seriously and believing women, Notley threw Luff out of caucus. Not the bullies. Not the intimidators. Not the MLAs accused of sexual misconduct. They got to stay in caucus. Notley blamed the victim and punished her by throwing her out of caucus. Luff sits as an independent now.

But other complaints emerged, too, including allegations of sexual misconduct. Notley arranged for a confidential in-party investigation into those cases and found that two of her MLAs needed intervention. But she controlled the entire process: She refused to publicly give any details, or even name the MLAs she had disciplined. Here's how the NDP spun it: "The investigations concluded that the behaviour could be addressed through education and instruction… For the people who brought forward these complaints, the issues were serious, and — as in every case involving allegations of inappropriate behaviour — they needed to be heard and addressed."

So that was supposed to be it. Notley admitted there was a problem with sexual misconduct, but says she'll be keeping the ugly details to herself rather than letting voters in on exactly which MLAs are guilty of the troubling charges. It was a stunning message to her MLAs and their victims: that Notley's people are protected, even if they engage in misconduct. And that any women should think twice before complaining about powerful friends of Notley.

Amazingly, the rest of the Alberta media seemed more than happy to play along, letting Notley keep the whole thing hush-hush right through to the election campaign, rather than reporters, you know, trying to actually root out the men behind the sex scandal. Thankfully, The Rebel wasn't about to let that happen.

As my Rebel colleague Keean Bexte reported in February, we believe we were able to identify the two government MLAs who were investigated and disciplined by Notley for sexual misconduct.

Notley may use the flimsy excuse of not naming the perpetrators because she wants to ensure the complainants' privacy, but affidavits filed in public court documents suggest that there may be other reasons for Notley to keep things as under-wraps as possible: The

Rebel's investigation suggests the two MLAs involved are key Notley lieutenants.

According to documents filed at the Edmonton Court of Queen's bench, the two NDP MLAs who engaged in sexual misconduct are: Deron Bilous, the minister for economic development and trade and Edmonton MLA Heather Sweet, Notley's deputy chair of committees and chair of the NDP caucus. The misconduct appears to revolve around an affair between these two senior Notley deputies, which was cited by Bilous's wife in divorce proceedings.

Divorces are common, not least in a high-stress occupation like politics. Cheating is too, unfortunately. Neither of those troubles would normally rise to the level of a public-interest news story. Notley, Bilous and Sweet have stonewalled us, and refuse to directly answer whether this is the misconduct for which they were investigated, but it fits the facts that Notley's office has already confirmed: That the misconduct in question did not happen at work and the complainants were not staff. It sounds like a description of the divorce proceedings in this case, and it fits the timeline.

But Notley's office said after its investigation that the two MLAs in question — which would appear to be Bilous and Sweet — needed "education and instruction." Would a divorce, on its own, cause Notley to order MLAs to undergo education and instruction? If not, what else did they do? Is it what The Rebel uncovered in the Bilous divorce court documents?

Allegations made by a divorcing couple can be made in bitterness and rancour, and have to be taken with a grain of salt. But Bilous's estranged wife claims Bilous is a regular drug user —she even calls him an addict. The Rebel asked Bilous about that allegation but he did not respond to our requests. His estranged wife also claims in her filings that, at least on one occasion, a senior NDP staffer, named Heather Mack — the chief of staff to NDP MLA Sandra Jansen — actually went to court, to attend the divorce proceedings, in the middle of her government workday.

That's pretty weird. Why was an NDP staffer being sent to attend the hostile divorce proceedings of an NDP MLA and his wife? Was she doing it for Bilous? Was she acting for the NDP, to monitor what was said in court, for damage control? Was she there to intimidate Bilous's wife? We don't know — we asked her, but she didn't respond to our questions, either.

One thing we do know is this: Wikipedia logs any changes that anyone makes to a Wikipedia entry and shows it publicly, along with the IP address — the exact location on the Internet of the computer that made the changes. That's how the system at Wikipedia works. And on the Wikipedia entry for Daren Bilous, the logs show that someone from the NDP government had been changing information. And the address of the computer that had made those changes? Right inside the office of Heather Mack, the NDP chief of staff for MLA Sandra Jansen who was also at Bilous's court hearing.

The number of questions raised by all this is enough to make your head spin. Why is staff from the Notley government getting involved in the private divorce proceedings of an NDP MLA? What other pressure was Notley putting on women who complained about NDP MLAs? What other weird missions were being conducted with taxpayer resources and government staff?

That's why at least some of what is being alleged is of public interest. Not all of it, of course. The Rebel did not report on the vast majority of the material in Bilous's divorce proceedings. The private lives of citizens are not usually in the public interest. Even senior government officials deserve some privacy in their personal lives. Except in the most unusual circumstances, families of politicians are not fair game either. In our investigation, we learned a great deal about some NDP politicians, but we have chosen not to report most of it — it's simply not relevant to their public duties.

(By the way, when it comes to conservatives, the mainstream media is happy to ignore that rule and raid their privacy. The mainstream media widely reported it went Notley's war room tipped them that Opposition leader Jason Kenney for living for a period of time with his widowed mother after his dad died; they even published floor plans of the house. And left-wing media like *Vice* regularly "out" conservatives as gay, and have been gleefully suggesting that Kenney himself is, too. So much for respecting politicians' privacy and personal dignity.)

The Rebel's reporting on this case has stuck to matters of interest to the public. Like the allegations of a drug addiction. (That was the one part of the media frenzy about the late former mayor of Toronto, Rob Ford — whether he was impaired on the job and potentially at danger of being blackmailed or compromised because of his drug habit.)

And like this: According to the court documents, Bilous has refused to pay spousal support.

That matter was still before a judge when we exposed it. But is it not relevant to the public, when assessing the character of someone who proudly identifies as a male feminist? That his wife has to sue him for spousal support?

But what has the NDP done to protect the public interest during this whole ugly episode? Heather Sweet is an NDP government MLA, subordinate to a minister like Deron Bilous. But she's also the caucus chair, which gives her a certain power, too. Has Notley put in place any rules for managing the relationship between Bilous and Sweet? As an MLA, Sweet would be expected to represent her constituents' interests when petitioning ministries, especially one like Bilous's economic development and trade, which has the power to do favours (or not) for certain business, industries and regions?

How can the public be sure that Bilous is neither favouring, nor disfavouring, requests from his now former mistress, including for financial or other benefits? Was their personal relationship even disclosed to department staff, so they can ensure that no favouritism occurs?

Meanwhile, there's the matter of the allegations of Bilous's drug addiction and his refusal to support his estranged wife.

Shortly after Bilous and his wife split, and he had removed his belongings from their shared home, the house caught fire and burned to the ground, leaving Mrs. Bilous and her son without clothes or a roof. If it's true that Deron Bilous is refusing to help her with spousal support, that adds an even more troubling element to the matter of public interest.

Now, divorces can be acrimonious; complaints can be exaggerated. Maybe nothing that Mrs. Bilous has sworn in her affidavits, under pain of perjury is true. Maybe she legally doesn't have a right to spousal support, or to a share in the matrimonial home that is being rebuilt after the fire. She also accuses him of bullying. Maybe that's not true, either.

But a judge ordered Bilous to pay her support; he didn't. Her repeated requests were ignored, to the point where Mrs. Bilous went to court, asking a judge to find Bilous in contempt (and to immediately pay her back-support). Surely that is something relevant for voters to be aware of in the age of #MeToo, where progressives in the NDP, including Bilous himself, asks us to believe accusers.

And so is this: Deron Bilous's estranged wife says he has enough money, because, she alleges, he spends plenty on abusing substances. As she alleges in her filing: "This also included being engulfed in a lifestyle of drugs and alcohol wherein Mr. Bilous spent copious amounts of money on these addictions." His estranged wife says in the filing that she never engaged in that lifestyle herself and has even "refrained from including all details of their relationship which include Mr. Bilous's drinking and drug related lifestyle out of respect for him and for his career."

So, we have an affair between two high-ranking government MLAs that leads to acrimony, and apparently, a full-blown investigation. That's clearly a matter of public interest. So are affidavit-sworn allegations of drug addiction; so is government staff being sent to divorce hearings; and the very credibility of so-called feminist politicians who have a pattern of mistreating women. That's all news in the public interest. But that's the very news Notley didn't want Albertans to find out. It's a good thing we did.

In the weeks since we broke this story, not a single other mainstream journalist followed up on it, not even to the sworn affidavit by Mrs.

Bilous alleging drug abuse by a senior cabinet minister. It's a stark contrast to the flood-the-zone coverage of any foibles from politicians on the left, such as the late Toronto mayor, Rob Ford.

But it also raises the question: what other scandals has the NDP managed to keep under wraps from a lazy press gallery?

CHAPTER 8

"EXTREMELY VIOLENT AND BRUTAL"

It's hard to pinpoint the moment where Alberta's NDP went from being a party made up heavily of farmers to a party so unconnected to the land and the back country that there is literally not one single farmer in Notley's NDP caucus.

Just think about that. This is an Alberta government, with a 55-seat majority, in the very province where the NDP's predecessor, the Co-operative Commonwealth Federation, was founded in part by agrarian groups. In a province where there are still nearly 50,000 active farms — that's one for every 80 people in the province — and where 27 per cent of people in the province live in rural areas or small centres. And not a single farmer or rancher or anyone working the land among them? How is that even statistically possible? They've got seven teachers. They've got six social workers. They've got four union administrators. Three nurses. Heck, there are even three — *three* — NDP MLAs whose career before politics was simply "student." And two bus drivers. That's right. Not just one bus driver — two bus drivers! Of course there's nothing wrong with an honest day's work driving a bus. but how does a party get elected in a substantially rural Prairie province with not one single solitary farmer or rancher?

Nothing better demonstrates the wildly unbalanced way the NDP thinks and sees Alberta than the complete lopsidedness of its caucus. Yes, of course the province needs its social workers, teachers, students and nurses, and they should absolutely have a voice in government. But in this NDP, a whole lot of public sector workers and union shop stewards are the only voice in government. And that's how you end up with a government that somehow, amazingly, managed to provoke, of all things, public protests by … Hutterites.

Hutterite protests! It sounds almost like a joke. Like something you'd see in a comedy film. Hutterites — like other Christian farm communes, like the Amish in New England — are actually committed to being apolitical. These are people of the land who literally embrace Christian pacifism as one of their key tenets. Hutterites are into farming, milking cows, erecting barns, singing hymns and knitting — not marching in the street. They go to church pretty much every day. The women wear actual bonnets, for crying out loud. Who on earth could manage to get Hutterites angry enough to come out protest against the provincial government?

Rachel Notley's government, that's who.

Maybe the NDP didn't even realize there were Hutterites in Alberta. Hutterites live almost entirely in the rural area, where they live quietly, faithfully and peacefully off the land. The left-wing NDP public-sector class wouldn't have run into them much at their anti-oilsands rallies or their conferences on the intersectionality of race, gender and identity in late capitalist systems of authority.

Rachel Notley's first chief of staff, Brian Topp, was a Torontonian — ask him what a Hutterite is, and he'd probably guess that it was an element in the periodic table.

If you see Hutterites in the city at all, it might be at a truck dealership, or a farmer's market, with a bunch of sweet, apple-cheeked kids selling their farm produce — just as they do at the market stands you'll find in the countries, with those same kids ready to sell you baskets of fresh fruit and vegetables or fresh eggs.

But then Notley actually tried to tell the Hutterites that she was going to bring union rules to the family farm. Among the proposed rules was a plan to force farm families to treat their own children as "employees," providing them with insurance coverage and benefits. As one Worker's Compensation Board document said: "If you are operating a for-profit farming operation … you must cover any unpaid workers, including family members and children, performing work on your farm."

And that's how you get Hutterites to protest.

It's one thing not to understand life on the farm. If you've got a caucus of 55 people and not a single one of them has ever ploughed a field or harvested a crop, that's to be expected. It's a completely distorted reflection of Albertans, of course: Notley's NDP is more of a Socialist International solidarity society, with its students, public sector workers and union activists. But you'd at least think that would alert them that they should probably tread lightly before deciding they were going to completely overhaul the way farmers have to operate in the province. Maybe, before you start passing draconian new laws about forcing big labour union rules onto farms, you might hold a few town halls and meet some actual farmers and talk to them. Maybe then, you might not screw things up so colossally that you end up mobilizing even pacifist Hutterites into protest.

But the NDP had no interest in that. They had just taken power in 2015, and they were eager to put into practice the agricultural collectivization experiments that socialists have always had such great luck with. You just need to look at Stalin's Ukraine and Mao's China to see that when radical lefties try their hand at redesigning farming institutions that have been embedded human history for thousands of years, it doesn't end up well. But the next group is always sure it's going to get it right. And Notley's NDP was ready to take its shot.

In the immediate aftermath of their win, they got to work meeting with "stakeholders" to draft an omnibus farm safety legislation. Any normal government putting together a list of stakeholders to discuss farm policy might include, you know, farmers. How about just one rancher, even? Or how about just a simple chapter of the government's own 4-H program?

Come to think of it… do you think people on Notley's team had even ever heard of the 4-H program before they found it in their government portfolio?

Don't be silly. Besides, those aren't the kind of "stakeholders" they were interested in meeting with. They were consulting their friends in the Alberta Federation of Labor and social activists. Because they didn't care about protecting the family farm. They were out to increase the power of big labour and kill off the spirit of independence and self-reliance that has animated Alberta and has been building this province since before the NDP even existed. And they would do it with a brand new bill, Bill 6.

What was Bill 6? Oh, just a sweeping, disruptive and draconian bill of massive proportions that would create new labour laws and regulations that would put urban, union style rules on Alberta's nearly 50,000 farms. Bill 6 would actually open up 31 per cent of the total farm area in the country for unionization, and mandate onerous occupation health and safety regulations — including worker's compensation coverage. Without any input from actual people who know about actual farming and ranching, Bill 6 was replete with outrageous rules that risked actually killing off farms altogether: No longer could children work on the farm — that's what really got to the Hutterites, understandably. The Hutterites were completely forgotten and disregarded in Bill 6. In their culture, kids grow up working and learning the farm first hand. How many hours would the NDP permit those youngsters to work? And in a piece of legislation that divided farms into "employers" and "workers," who was who in a religion that dictates that they own all things in common? The government eventually offered to exempt the Hutterites; to their credit, these Albertans refused to be treated differently than their neighbours, and stood fast against Bill 6. They were not about to let a socialist government divide them from the other people in their communities where they live and where they do business. And besides, they were family farmers, too. No different than the rest of the worried farmers in Alberta who were under attack.

That wasn't all that upset farmers: Any firearms, which farmers use to scare off cougars, bears and other predators away from their livestock, could no longer be on a "work site" — which was the NDP's new socialist union term for what the rest of us call "family farms." And a whole whack of new rules for overtime and hours of work completely disregarded the realities of when harvest, calving, lambing, and planting happens in real life on real farms.

Bill 6 would be a massive accomplishment for Notley's cronies in the labour movement, a huge get with lot of potential for increased union dues, and most damagingly of all, by converting independent family farms into government-regulated union worksites, it would advance Notley's plan for the increased socialization of a free-enterprise province into a public-sector-dominated big government welfare state.

And the NDP climate crusaders who are so obsessed with weather and warming when they're at their anti-oilsands rallies, when they're celebrating punitive carbon taxes and when they're sloshing millions of dollars of public money around into 'green' projects that go nowhere, somehow failed to grasp that on the farm, climate isn't just a slogan, it's a major factor of production. That farmers are truly at the whims of nature. That working long days is sometimes non-optional, when the crops need to be brought in and there's a frost coming or a storm blowing in. That they have to make hay when the sun shines, not when labour regulations say it's legal to do so.

The law was a shocking, outrageous and glaring symbol of how Notley's urban, activist-class NDP has no grasp of the culture of rural Alberta — of a culture where a neighbour might come help pull a calf at 2 a.m. and not expect a thing in return except maybe a little help some time changing a tire on a baler. The NDP didn't understand that you just can't forcibly impose union regulations on the hours and work conditions of neighbourliness.

And that's why no one in the NDP caucus of students, teachers, bus drivers and social workers anticipated that farmers might hate it so much that they would rise up in protest.

Rallies sprang up. Thousands of farmers. Convoys of tractors stretching kilometres down major highways. As one protester told the *National Post* about Notley's plan, "She is going to make every single farm and ranch go bankrupt." The farmers were clear: They weren't against improving farm safety, which the NDP claimed Bill 6 was supposed to be about. They were against trying to improve farm safety by imposing rules that were totally ignorant of the realities of life on a farm. "I think a reasonable government would have come out and said, 'Hey, do you want to make these places safer?' and they'd have gotten a pat on the back and a 'show me a way,' " one farmer said.

And how did the tone-deaf NDP respond? By painting farmers as reckless extremists who didn't care about safety and weren't interested in treating workers fairly. After one peaceful demonstration, where children joined in, NDP cabinet minister Shaye Anderson called the rally "extremely violent and brutal." They weren't interested in listening to farmers before and they weren't about to listen to farmers even now. Even as tractors rolled, and the protests built, the NDP just went ahead and passed their bill, using the trick of invoking closure in the legislature, to cut off any more democratic debate about it.

That kind of disdain and anti-democratic refusal to listen to Alberta's rural communities is how the NDP would govern through the rest of its term. It reared its ugly head again most visibly in September 2015, when out of the blue the NDP announced they were creating a pair of new parks — one provincial and the other a "wilderness park" — in the Castle region near Crowsnest Pass. Notley's government insisted protecting these 105,000 hectares of land was the best way to preserve grizzly and cutthroat trout habitat for future generations while still allowing backcountry-loving Albertans to continue to use the land the way they always had — for hunting, fishing, hiking, off-roading and wilderness camping. It was all a lie.

Environment Minister Shannon Phillips even sent a hand notated letter to the president of the local off-highway vehicle (OHV) group, the Crowsnest Pass Quad Squad, to assure them that they would still be welcome in the new provincial park. She even thanked them for all they had already done to keep Castle protected and clean.

As it would turn out, Phillips's assurance would mean nothing. It wasn't worth the paper it was written on. The NDP would betray the off-roaders entirely, announcing that they would be banning OHVs from the new park entirely because the machines were bad for the environment. The government vilified the off-roaders: They were ruining the headwaters, killing the fish, and making an all around mess, they said.

That, too, was a lie. In fact, no one had been more careful and more invested in preserving the backcountry than the off-road groups who loved it. They had been clearing trails to go around vulnerable eco-systems. They had raised thousands of dollars in donated labour and materials to build bridges over streams. They had spent endless hours voluntarily picking up garbage left behind by others.

But the lying and vilification was necessary for Notley's radical NDPers because they needed an excuse to impose what it turned out was a foreign-funded effort to block any more development in Alberta. The same kind of effort that was behind the blockade of Alberta oil, called the Yellowstone to Yukon, or Y2Y, initiative that helped push the creation of a whole new "sacred" area in B.C., the Great Bear Rainforest, which was invented entirely by eco-warriors and would become their excuse, adopted by the federal Trudeau Liberal government, to block Albertan oil pipelines to the coast.

According to researcher Vivian Krause, who has for years meticulously traced the flow of foreign money into anti-Alberta initiatives, "the biggest funder of the Y2Y is the Wilburforce Foundation, funded by James Letwin, a co-founder of Microsoft. Back in 2004, Wilburforce stipulated that the purpose of funding Y2Y was to protect vast tracts of the Western U.S. and Canada "from oil and gas development, through an advocacy campaign that focuses on grizzly bears and critical wildlife habitat," tax returns say. It has granted more than US$25 million to environmental and other anti-developments groups in Western Canada. That includes groups like the Canadian Parks and Wilderness Society, one of the main groups behind the NDP's plan to turn the Castle region off-limits to the Albertans who have used it and cared for it for so long.

The next unwanted park being offered up to please the NDP's foreign-funded anti-development activist friends is the Bighorn Backcountry. The Bighorn is also part of the Eastern Slopes and there is a lot of oil and gas development in the region benefitting the region's towns and First Nations. But like with the Castle plan, the land-use changes in the Bighorn will make an enormous portion of Western Alberta off limits to the people who live there and use it every day. What are currently public lands for use of the public will be rezoned, just like Castle, to become a provincial park with similar restrictions on hunting, fishing, random camping, ATV use and potentially oil and gas development and logging.

But after having burnt so many bridges and engendered so much ill will with Alberta's backcountry lovers and rural communities, the NDP suddenly ran into more opposition than it expected over Bighorn. People began organizing against it, like with the farm bill, and the NDP could see another public relations catastrophe on their hands as average, rural Albertans peacefully stood up to their extremist agenda.

They began mobilizing, holding rallies with speakers from off highway vehicle associations, hunting and guiding organizations and Indigenous groups, like the Sunchild First Nation. Sunchild Councillor Joey Pete told a crowd of several hundred in Red Deer that his people didn't need the NDP telling his First Nations people how to care for and protect the land. Notley's government had claimed they had thoroughly consulted the Sunchild band on the plan and their concerns; Pete denied that there had been any meaningful consultation with his band at all. But the bogus stories coming from the NDP on this alarming plan were just getting started.

With anger rising and people demanding answers, the next outrageous move was for Environment Minister Shannon Phillips to cancel the public consultations, cutting off any more democratic discussion of the matter. Incredibly, she issued a press release blaming opponents for — once again — being violent and dangerous. It read:

"I have heard stories of Albertans afraid to attend community events, Albertans berated in public, Albertans followed home, and Albertans feeling intimidated to not speak their mind or participate in this important discussion. These reports are not only deeply concerning, this behaviour is not reflective of the values we all share. I call on all of my elected colleagues to denounce the bullying and harassment being faced by Bighorn supporters.

"As we do not feel we can guarantee the public's safety or freedom from intimidation at this time, I am very disappointed to announce that the upcoming sessions for Drayton Valley, Red Deer, Sundre and Edmonton will be cancelled."

Except none of that was true, either.

The *Calgary Herald's* Licia Corbella investigated these supposed threats and intimidation. She contacted Constable Mike Hibbs, the media relations officer for Alberta's RCMP K Division's southern district. And what do you know? Hibbs said that he hadn't heard of a single threats or possible danger. "I'm not aware of anything — of any threats at all," Hibbs said.

And yet, instead of apologizing and clearing the matter up, Phillips, unbelievably, doubled down. She told reporters that she had indeed received advice from the RCMP and security officials, along with reports of harassment. That, she said, had prompted the government to cancel the open houses.

But then when reporters looked into that claim, it too seemed entirely fabricated when Fraser Logan of the RCMP said the police service did not provide any official advice on security at the open houses.

Phillips had lied again.

And still, she kept spinning her baseless stories. In a subsequent teleconference with reporters, Phillips said the RCMP were investigating at least two complaints. She said: "I know that there are at least two open investigation — open files — with file investigation numbers, with respect to allegations of safety concerns for the public in and around, in central Alberta.

You would think she would have learned that police weren't going to back up her baloney. And once again, the Mounties busted her lies wide open. They issued a statement to the press clearly stating that "Alberta RCMP can confirm that we do not have any ongoing investigations relating to the consultations"

There were no threats. There was no danger. The only thing Phillips was afraid of was the very public she was supposed to be listening to and representing as a minister of the provincial government. But she wasn't interested in what actual Albertans had to say. She didn't want to hear that they were upset, that her policies were harming them. She wasn't doing this for them; she was doing this for her radical environmentalist friends using money from billion-dollar foundations to block development in Alberta, regardless of what Albertans themselves wanted. And so she took a page out of the same playbook that Shaye Anderson used to discredit and dismiss the concerns of farmers, when he called their protests "extremely violent and brutal." She slandered them. She vilified them. She made it sound like these regular people with legitimate concerns were unhinged and dangerous. All as a way to shut down the democratic process, to stifle any dissent or debate, and to ram through anti-Albertan policies backed by anti-Albertan foreign groups. That's who Phillips, Notley and the NDP really serve. And as far as they're concerned, actual Albertans had better just sit down, shut up and take it.

CHAPTER 9

EPILOGUE

It's been a catastrophic four years for Alberta under the NDP. There really is no other way to describe what has happened here. An utter catastrophe.

A rag-tag NDP cadre made up of the inept and the malicious, some imported and some local, did their best to undo Alberta. They didn't want to understand the culture of rugged individualism and entrepreneurship that sent people streaming into Alberta for freedom and work for generations.

They wanted those dirty farmers and icky righands to be more like the people in their favorite boutique coffee shops, with their egg-shaped cars and their electric bikes. They just needed a gentle nudge in the right direction, and if that didn't work then the NDP would use a hammer.

The NDP tried to remake the place. And they nearly succeeded.

According to the Office of the Superintendent of Bankruptcy, 14,700 Albertans declared personal insolvency in 2018, a nearly 10% increase from the year before and the second highest increase among Canadian provinces after Newfoundland and Labrador.

March 2018 unemployment statistics ranked Calgary at the highest in the entire nation at 7.6%, jumping ahead of St. John's, Newfoundland at 7.4%.

Co-conspirators Notley and Trudeau have overseen the evacuation of investment capital at a rate never seen before. According to a report by JWN Energy, "$100 billion worth of energy projects were killed, canceled or stalled, according to a new report by the C.D. Howe Institute. That is equivalent to 4.5% of Canada's gross domestic product."

At the very same time, oil and gas investment in other jurisdictions is increasing. The United States, with their energy friendly president, saw a 50% increase in energy investment in 2017 alone.

No one has any confidence in Notley's Alberta. The Fraser Institute's Global petroleum survey ranks Alberta as one of the least attractive places for oil and gas investment. Alberta dropped from 33rd (out of 97) in 2017 to 43rd (out of 80) in 2018. And get this: More than 50% of survey respondents see Alberta's fiscal terms and taxation as deterrents to investment. Translation: they don't like Notley's carbon tax and corporate tax hike.

Let's be honest. It is bleak out there. People have lost everything and others are just treading water. Towns are suffering and businesses are shuttering.

But it's nearly over if the polls are correct. It's a time for optimism again. No, really.

Alberta is a fruitful place and the people aren't easy to break. Smarter politicians have tried.

Because while governments and politicians change, some things remain constant. Albertans know the value of the Prairie work ethic, that hard work self-reliance and a strong sense of community leave little room for government interference. That much about Alberta, the NDP couldn't change, no matter how hard they tried these last four years.

And Alberta has faced hard times before. In 1993, Alberta's debt-servicing costs amounted to 33% of the healthcare budget. Through hard work, tough decisions, and strong leadership, Alberta got back on track.

When Justin Trudeau's father's National Energy Program nearly destroyed the oil patch in his attempt to bring Alberta to its knees, Alberta fought back, eventually becoming the economic powerhouse of Confederation.

The moral of the story is you can't keep Alberta down for long.

It's something late premier Ralph Klein believed about us, too.

"This is a province rich in blessings and hope. The best is yet to come!"

40043089R00052

Made in the USA
Middletown, DE
25 March 2019